ROMAN WOMEN

This richly illustrated book examines the daily lives of Roman women by focusing on the mundane and less-celebrated aspects of daily life – family and household, work and leisure, worship and social obligations – of women of different social ranks. Using a variety of sources, including literary texts, letters, inscriptions, coins, tableware, furniture, and the fine arts, from the late republic to the high imperial period, Eve D'Ambra shows how these sources serve as objects of social analysis, rather than simply as documents that re-create how life was lived. She also demonstrates how texts and material objects take part in shaping realities and what they can tell us about the texture of lives and social attitudes, if not the emotions of women in Roman antiquity.

Eve D'Ambra is Professor and Chair of the Department of Art at Vassar College. She is the author of *Roman Art* (Cambridge, 1998).

CAMBRIDGE INTRODUCTION TO ROMAN CIVILIZATION

Cambridge Introduction to Roman Civilization is a program of books designed for use by students who have no prior knowledge of or familiarity with Roman antiquity. Books in this series focus on key topics, such as slavery, warfare, and women. They are intended to serve as a first point of reference for students who will then be equipped to seek more specialized scholarly and critical studies. Texts in these volumes are written in clear, jargon-free language and will integrate scholarship primary texts into a synthetics that reflects the most up-to-date research. All volumes in the series will be closely linked to readings and topics presented in the Cambridge Latin Course.

ROMAN WOMEN

EVE D'AMBRA
Vassar College

CAMBRIDGE
UNIVERSITY PRESS

CAMBRIDGE
UNIVERSITY PRESS

University Printing House, Cambridge CB2 8BS, United Kingdom

One Liberty Plaza, 20th Floor, New York, NY 10006, USA

477 Williamstown Road, Port Melbourne, VIC 3207, Australia

4843/24, 2nd Floor, Ansari Road, Daryaganj, Delhi - 110002, India

79 Anson Road, #06-04/06, Singapore 079906

Cambridge University Press is part of the University of Cambridge.

It furthers the University's mission by disseminating knowledge in the pursuit of education, learning and research at the highest international levels of excellence.

www.cambridge.org
Information on this title: www.cambridge.org/9780521521581

© Cambridge University Press 2007

First published 2007

A catalogue record for this publication is available from the British Library

Library of Congress Cataloging in Publication data
D'Ambra, Eve, 1956–
Roman women / Eve D'Ambra.
p.   cm. – (Cambridge introduction to Roman civilization)
Includes bibliographical references.
ISBN-13: 978-0-521-81839-1 (hardcover)
ISBN-10: 0-521-81839-7 (hardcover)
ISBN-13: 978-0-521-52158-1 (pbk.)
ISBN-10: 0-521-52158-0 (pbk.)
1. Women – Rome – Social conditions.   I. Title.   II. Series.
HQ1136.D35   2006
305.48'871 – dc22   2005036464

ISBN 978-0-521-81839-1 Hardback
ISBN 978-0-521-52158-1 Paperback

To My Mother and My Daughter

CONTENTS

LIST OF MAPS AND ILLUSTRATIONS

ACKNOWLEDGMENTS

This is a brief book on a large and increasingly unwieldy subject. In the course of its composition, I have imagined it as being perched atop a pile of scholarship, some of it quite hefty and other parts gossamer light. The book, of course, bears the imprint of the work of many fine scholars of previous generations who ventured into what was once new territory. Now the subject of Roman women seems rather more familiar, if not completely exhausted. By surveying topics that revolve around the concept and realities of Roman women, I have aimed to make these accessible to introductory students and laymen while avoiding some of the boilerplate of the genre. The juxtaposition of text and images offers a collage that may foil our impulse to match facts and pictures, a craving too often satisfied in textbooks. The images are taken seriously as sources of evidence, even when they contradict or only relate obliquely to ancient literary or historical sources. Amid the touchstones and major monuments required of such a venture, my discussions ought to suggest the depth and complexity of the issues without bringing it all to the surface. Attention is given to the ordinary and everyday aspects of life rather than to the spectacular and cinematic scenery of ancient Rome. No book is written without a point of view, and my preferences for the plebeian and anticlassical are apparent throughout.

A number of institutions have supported my work along the way. Research begun during a Howard Foundation fellowship from Brown University wound up in several chapters. I completed a draft of the book while on a sabbatical supported by the John Simon Guggenheim Foundation and the National Endowment for the Humanities, which provided stretches of time for reading and thinking. A leave from Vassar College and the Lucy Shoe Meritt Residency in Ancient Studies at the American Academy in Rome brought me back to the city and its many pleasures. A summer seminar offered by the National Endowment for the Humanities on Roman Egypt at Columbia University proved to be important, and I thank Roger Bagnall for introducing me to this area. Sheila Dillon and Sharon James set their accomplished students on me during a stimulating visit to their seminar on women in antiquity at Duke University and the University of North Carolina at Chapel Hill.

I am grateful for my editor at Cambridge University Press, Beatrice Rehl, who offered me the opportunity to write this book and who provided clear-eyed advice along the way. She had the foresight to bring on Lisa Swyers as a photo editor whose patience and perseverance are boundless. I thank Hans Rupprecht Goette for his advice and his digital photo archives that he made available to us. Steve Vinson generously took time away from his research leave to photograph mummy portraits in the Cairo Museum. Naomi J. Norman offered slides of the reliefs from La Marsa in the Carthage Museum. Judith Barringer, Eleanor Winsor Leach, Christine Kondoleon, and Bettina Bergmann also pointed us in the right direction for the acquisition of photos.

I also thank the anonymous reader for the Press for improving the manuscript in many small but significant ways. Jacqueline Musacchio of Vassar College sharpened the prose of a preliminary chapter and asked important questions. Harriet Flower read part of the manuscript and advised on matters of history and religion. Eleanor Winsor Leach read a couple of chapters and prodded me to return to some literary passages. Barbara Kellum fielded questions on slavery, and Matthew Roller did likewise on an inscription. Sinclair Bell provided bibliographic references and tracked books down in European libraries. Judith Barringer, as always, provided moral support and counsel on the big picture. I have tried to incorporate all of their wise suggestions but, of course, any remaining errors, distortions, or omissions are all my own doing.

Vassar College was instrumental in providing student research assistants who have made the work a pleasure. The Ford Foundation supported Christine Wegner's summer research that started the project, and Christine may have gotten more out of this than we both realized. Rachel Kozinn served admirably, and Courtney Biggs provided exemplary assistance in seeing the book through to the end with a sense of humor. Kathryn Madden not only assisted in fact-checking, but produced the index on a tight schedule. I thank them for their hard work and attention to detail. Thomas Hill of Vassar's Art Library supplied a steady stream of cappuccino and bibliographic assistance. Ellic Davies and Liliana Aguis also helped out in the library and office. I was not alone in this endeavor – neither at the office nor at home, where my husband and daughter distracted me in ways that allowed my mind to wander and then come back, refreshed.

Poughkeepsie
January 2005

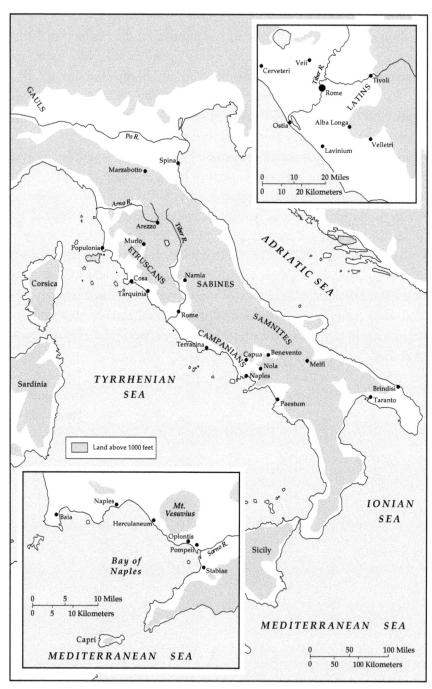

Italy in the third–second centuries B.C.

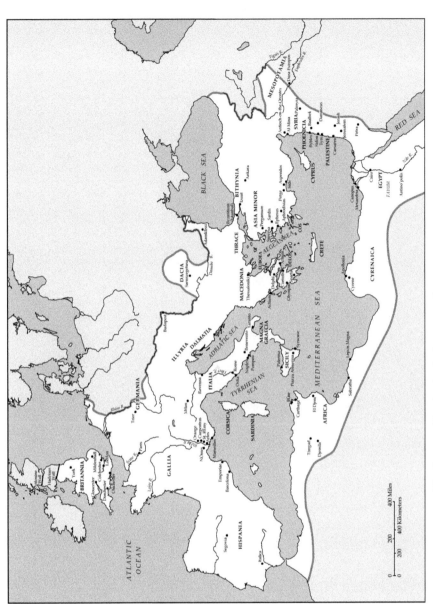

The Roman Empire in the late second century C.E.

CHAPTER 1

—

GENDER AND STATUS

Being a woman in ancient Rome bears only *some* resemblance to the current range of experiences available to women. Students of classics and history tend to see continuities in the importance given to marriage and family, home and hearth, yet the Roman institutions that shaped lives were fundamentally different than those of postmodern society. For example, a young Roman woman married a man of her parents' choosing and later divorced if her parents thought it advisable, and both of these milestones were accomplished with the minimum of legal procedures (if one possessed the legal capacity to marry, then consent to marry was required, along with the performance of ritual acts; divorce was rather an informal affair marked by the wife leaving the husband's house and the return of her dowry, if merited). The stories of the first marriages in Rome told of women abducted by their future husbands, acts that are not only incompatible with girls' visions of romantic love but also criminal in most contemporary societies. Some Roman lives seem familiar to us from tales of wifely virtue and heroic action, but we must realize how every aspect of their world reinforced a social system based on inequality and elitism. Its institutions and culture were also configured in a way that may disorient or confuse us: what we consider private and public did not conform to Roman definitions, and their spheres of work and leisure, politics and administration, included activities that would strain our understanding of these categories. Rediscovering Roman women requires an ability to mine the ancient source material with imagination firmly grounded in social reality.

Sources

Histories of Roman women have tended to set them apart, as if one could get a sense of their lives without dealing with men (but, of course, it was their dependence on fathers and husbands that has obscured their identities). Partly this isolation results from the intent to give the silent women of Rome the attention they merit and to restore their voices to the historical record. Yet, these accounts have tended to elevate the exceptional, larger-than-life characters and events that stand out from everyday life, which pales in comparison. Another trend in earlier studies was to cast Roman matrons as the liberated ladies of antiquity compared with the more retiring and sheltered women of Greece, for example. Although Roman women had citizenship and powers over their property, their freedom and well-being were contingent on their relationships with husbands and fathers and their social class; in other words, they were not free agents. In part, the older scholarship has taken its cues from the ancient sources that characteristically note differences from the norm rather than explain what remained obvious to the ancient reader.

This book is about how Roman women lived with an emphasis on the mundane and less-celebrated aspects of daily life, that is, family and household, work and leisure, worship, and social obligations of women of different social ranks. The evidence is culled from written sources (both literary and nonliterary texts, such as letters and inscriptions), material culture (coins, tableware, furniture, etc.), and the fine arts in the periods from the late republic through the high empire (mostly from the first century B.C.E. through the second century C.E.). The ancient sources, both verbal and visual, are discussed as objects of social analysis rather than simply as documents of how life was lived. Some objects, such as ceramic cups, may give us a sense of their use; others, such as poems or sculpted portraits, may not reflect reality directly or transparently (laments over of a young girl's death, images of radiant beauty, etc.) but rather project specific points of view or ideals that reveal how Romans *imagined* their world. In other words, such texts or objects take part in *shaping* realities and can elicit the texture of lives and social attitudes, if not traces of emotions. Particularly because women do not speak to us directly in the ancient sources (exceptions noted in the following), it is important to determine who is representing them and for what purposes.

For example, clothing, as a purely functional object of everyday life that protected the wearer from the elements, was invested with symbolic value. According to some literary texts, dress distinguished respectable women from those without shame. The costume connoting the modesty of matrons (that is, married women of good standing) required the *stola*, after interpreted as a long garment hung from shoulder straps and reaching to the toes (a tunic was worn under it). There are some, but not many, statues that depict the *stola* dated to the late first and early first centuries B.C.E. to C.E. The problems lie with the archaeological evidence: fragments of cloth survive, mostly from the deserts of Roman Egypt and dating to late antiquity or the medieval period (rather than the periods of the republic and empire that concerns us). Otherwise, clothing is depicted in works of art, carved on statues, or portrayed in paintings, media that are not well suited to display the sheen of Coan (shot) silk nor its rustle in passing, despite some sculptors' virtuoso skills in carving layers of drapery wafting around a graceful figure. The poet Propertius addresses his mistress: "What good is it, promenading that way, your coiffure amazing, your couture an impressive shimmer of Coan silk as your skirts swing this way and that?" (1.2.1–3, trans. D. Slavitt). The iridescent quality of the fabric made its wearer appear sexy and desirable. The cost of such luxury, no doubt, also increased its allure for both the clotheshorse and her admirers. It is not easy to identify fabrics, let alone garments, depicted in works of art. Rather than mortal women, Venus, the goddess of sensuality and beauty, was more likely to exhibit clinging and filmy drapery in statue types (and she appears as a resplendent vision in myth). The goddess, however, had no shame, but these women in silk have been cast by scholars as either daring creatures who defied traditional codes of conduct or as pawns in a system that defined them as the "other" (as compared with the elite male) and trivialized their concerns for their appearance.

We have even less visual evidence of the matron's polar opposite, the prostitute. Women of easy virtue were thought to wear the male uniform of the toga as a reversal of the norm and, perhaps, to declare their bodies to be in the public domain. The togate (toga-wearing) prostitute is not depicted in art, and for good reason – statues of women were erected by their husbands and fathers to honor them for their exemplary roles as wives and mothers. Women who traded sex for money were not worthy of the medium of costly marble statues and, thus, were excluded from this prestigious form of representation.

1. Naples, Museo Archeologico Nazionale, inv. 9022, from Herculaneum. Erich
Lessing/Art Resource, N.Y., 16856. Painting of a woman's toilette, early first
century C.E. The scene is divided in half with two women watching the third being
dressed by her attendant. The costumes of tunics and mantles display silvery pastel
tones of yellow, blue, and pink with a more elaborate lower border on the tunic of
the woman being preened. In keeping with the literary sources on the female dress
code, the seated matron wears a veil; yet, it allows her to display much of her
swept-up hairstyle. All attention is on the delicate operation of styling the hair.

In other words, several literary accounts set up a rigid hierarchy
of appearances with dress codes. It is debatable whether these were so
strictly followed in life: in the visual arts respectable women often wore
simple tunics and mantles instead of the honorary *stola* and other groups
of women are not identifiable at all by costume (Figure 1). The same
authors who promoted the traditional and modest *stola* also inform us
that women covered their heads with their mantles when outside; yet,
many portrait statues and busts depict women with heads unveiled to

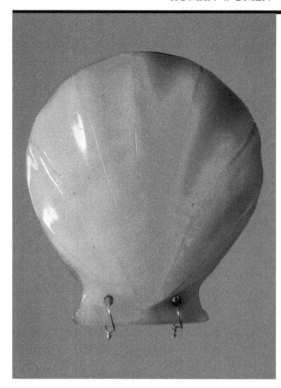

2. Rome, Museo Nazionale Romano, inv. 2005048. Compact in the form of a shell, mid-second century C.E. The hinged compact is made of amber, its lower half hollowed out to hold makeup or other cosmetics. As an allusion to Venus rising from the sea, the shell playfully invokes the goddess's powers over feminine rituals of adornment.

display showy, complex hairstyles (see Chapter 3). The male authors of the texts that have dominated our view of Roman women advanced standards of womanly behavior that best served the interests of patriarchy. Such representations of Roman women deployed a conventional or stereotypical language that cast women as weak, vain, and inherently amoral creatures. The litany of complaints against the female citizenry produced a steady, monotonous drone only broken by praise for the rare woman who exhibited the male virtues of self-control, discipline, and devotion to the greater good of the state. Neither the texts prescribing the female dress code nor the gleaming statuary depicting women draped from head to toe reflected reality in a truthful nor comprehensive way – rather, they provided models of ideal behavior for elite women to follow and, in this function, served as part of the ideological cultural apparatus that sought to control wives and mothers. That these ideals were highly contentious to some and did not reach their targeted audience is evident in the archaeological finds that suggest alternate ways of dressing up and looking like a woman.

In fact, both written sources (although a wider range of texts needs to be consulted) and archaeological material attest to the prevalence of the feminine arts of adornment and beautification. Fabrics were dyed brilliant hues in a spectrum from sky blue and sea green to saffron and amethyst purple (Ovid, *Ars Amatoria* 3.169–192). Gold jewelry was in demand, and gemstones could be imitated in paste for those without fortunes to spend. Recipes for makeup and cosmetics ran the gamut from homespun ingredients to impossibly exotic concoctions (Figures 2 and 3; see also Chapter 3). Despite the moralizing against adornment as a luxury and a precursor to vice in the literature (see Chapter 2), the archaeological record with its perfume jars and cosmetic containers suggests that many Roman women carefully crafted their looks. They sought beauty that would grace their appearances with sophistication and dignity.

3. Rome, Antiquarium Comunale, inv. 15123. Clay Lamp Depicting a Woman Bathing, mid-second century C.E. The lamp depicts an image in relief of a nude woman, crouching in the posture of a well-known statue of the bathing Venus. She is being washed by water pouring from a vase propped over her back, and she holds a small shell – are we to imagine this as a vision of the goddess or a depiction of a mortal woman merely posing provocatively as Venus? Figures 2 and 3 suggest how mythology permeated everyday life in aspects as banal as hygiene and beauty regimens.

As we see, the evidence offers varying accounts, which depend on the type or genre of the evidence in question, its author or producer, and intended audience. At times the evidence offered by visual and written sources does not match (as in the moralizing texts written for male readers and women's cosmetic compacts kept handy for spur-of-the-moment primping), and there may even be contradictions within the same general category of material objects or texts that invite questions about function or social context. Representations are not transparent renderings of the past "as it was" but constructions that, although grounded in specific social situations, do not document reality in a straightforward and obvious manner. The refinement and craftsmanship of Roman art and literature may seduce us into believing in the reality it invokes, but the representations did not mirror their world without distorting it or even negating it entirely.

For example, in the late first and early second centuries C.E., satire portrayed wealthy and spoiled women running their households and lording it over their husbands while funerary epitaphs inscribed on tombstones only tell of virtuous and obedient wives (Juvenal, *Satire* 6, and see, for example, the so-called Laudatio Turiae, *CIL* 6.1527, although this matron also boasts heroic action on behalf of her family). The difference can be attributed to the literary genre because satire demanded a broad target, usually marginal characters or the occasional big shot ready to be deflated, to attack ruthlessly; the epitaph commemorating a deceased and beloved wife served to praise her and preserve the memory of her goodness. Both genres also appeal to various audiences: satire was geared toward a sophisticated circle of insiders and conservatives who enjoyed the put downs of less well-entrenched groups or one of their own who has strayed (although there were also the obscene puns or drinking songs of the army and lower social orders), while the epitaphs were read by the extended family who gathered at the tomb and by curious passersby. Which view is correct? Both have to do with expectations of their genre and social attitudes: on the one hand, satire traded in cynicism and anger, exploiting fears of a world – or the drawing room – out of control that required remedy in keeping uppity women and other dangerous types down; on the other hand, the somber final words cut in stone evoked the respect and obligation owed to the dead and summoned the ideals and high sentiments to which families aspired. The biting humor of satire can be notoriously hard to translate from distant cultures, while the formulaic phrases of epitaphs are numbing in their repetition of abstract virtues and qualities that may ring hollow to us. Both sources have to be highly qualified as evidence for women's lives because the male satirists and mourning husbands had a stake in these representations of women; their underlying agenda often had little to do with the realities of Roman women, as we shall see.

Marriage by Capture

The stories Romans told about their origins are littered with abandoned wives and expendable mothers: Aeneas lost his wife, Creusa, during his flight from Troy and must leave her behind in the burning city (Virgil, *Aeneid*, 2.780–89); Romulus and Remus were begotten from a priestess, a Vestal Virgin, but were raised by a she-wolf. The myth, however, that set out the problems of marriage is the rape of the Sabine women: since Romulus needed women as wives for the first citizens of Rome, he invited a neighboring people, the Sabines (from an area northeast of Rome, see Map –), for a festival, and then abducted their women (Figure 4). Realizing that his venture would profit from the cooperation of the outraged and embittered women, Romulus addressed them on the protocols of Roman marriage: wives shared in their husbands' possessions–citizenship and children being the most prized; furthermore, he advised them to get over their anger and "give their hearts to those whom fortune had given their persons" (Livy 1.9.15–16, trans. B. Foster). In turn, the Romans would make good husbands, consoling their wives and reconciling them to their situation. The women lived with their Roman husbands as wives and fulfilled their conjugal duties. Later when their Sabine menfolk invaded Rome to reclaim their daughters and sisters, the Sabine women interceded between the battle lines to stop the fighting – they declared that they were now wives of the Romans and should stay in their new homes in Rome. The myth represents the women as outsiders, assimilated Romans, who made peace not only between the competing interests of family and the state but forged a community of Romans and Sabines. We may find it striking that the Sabine women came to identify with their captors, their Roman husbands, rather than with their Sabine fathers and brothers (Livy 1.9–13; see also Ovid, *Ars Amatoria* 1.99–134). Yet versions of the myth, which begin by treating the women as nonpersons, little more than the spoils of war, wind up elevating them as ambassadors who rise to the occasion by speaking for the greater good of both peoples. Rather than pleading as shrill victims, the Sabine women express a high-minded and enlightened position based on good citizenship, moral courage, and the mutual benefits of reconciliation.

This founding myth provides a blueprint for Roman attitudes toward women, marriage, and the imperial mission of conquest. Members of the female gender were valued according to age, status group, and moral character. Girls of leading families were kept close to home under constant supervision until they were handed over to husbands, usually mature or older men, selected by their elders. Once a maiden crossed the threshold of marriage and became a mother and matron, she assumed dignity and a public voice, as witnessed in the Sabine women. Aristocratic married women participated to some extent in public life because of their possession of sterling civic virtues that seemed to have been drummed into the offspring of noble families (see Chapter 4). The myth about the shrouded primeval origins of the city and empire, of course, suggests a world distant from the working-class quarters of imperial Rome in which marriage only seemed to grant endless work and self-sacrifice with no rewards or glory (see Chapter 3).

Furthermore, the myth also demonstrates how relationships born in violence, such as those resulting from Rome's confrontations with its neighbors, could develop into honorable unions. Even the non-Roman was convinced of the wisdom of merging with the empire, rather than resisting it. The transformation of the Sabine women from violated maidens carried off against their will to proactive and formidable citizens of

4. Rome, Antiquarium of the Roman Forum, photo DAI, Rome, 1939.722. Relief panel depicting the Rape of the Sabine Women, Rome, first century B.C.E.; the well-rounded bodies and swirling drapery suggest heroic action in progress with the effects of high drama. The panel is only one of a series that represented a narrative cycle of the founding moments of Roman history and was installed in a public building in the Roman Forum. The poet Propertius commented on the ubiquity of this story in children's lessons: "I don't have to mention the sordid business, that rape we all heard about as children before we knew what rape was" (4.10. 9–12, trans. D. Slavitt).

Rome occurred after they listened to Romulus's morale-building speech on the ideals of Roman marriage and accepted their lot in life as wives of men determined to do well by them. This civility (after the initial terror, we assume) was returned in kind: the Sabine women defended their commitment to their newly formed families (a characteristic of elite Roman women). In the myth marriage served as the institution not only to produce new citizens but also to convert foreigners into Romans (or, at least, to burden Sabines with Roman interests in their union) to increase the empire's dominion through the alleged superiority of its civilization. Marriage linked private life with political strategy in this example, and the absorption of foreign peoples into the empire was retailed as a partnership, rather than as conquest with the usual bloody repercussions. The household, thereafter, was a microcosm of the empire.

Gender and Power

Gender fit into a hierarchical system in which the male was superior, the female inferior and likened to other weak and wayward creatures, such as the non-Roman, the young, and untamed animals, all of whom required the firm hand of Roman male authority. According to medical authorities who could only consider the male form as achieving perfection, the female body was inherently defective. Maidens, young women physically developed and ready for marriage in their teens, required the most supervision because their budding sexuality left them vulnerable to physical desires that they might not be able to control. Female sexual desire was considered a dangerous, antisocial force by male authorities who saw it as a base appetite better suited to animals than humans. Yet female fertility was crucial to a society with high rates of infant mortality and childhood disease (see Chapter 2), and the nubile maiden was the bearer of the next generation. Marriage solved the problem – in theory, the earlier, the better for elite daughters, while others married later (in their upper teens or early twenties) and had to run the gauntlet of adolescent crises and a hostile environment with less protection. Marriage completed the female, invested her with a social presence, and saved her from her innate incompetence. The female biological role in reproduction weighed heavily in this system, which was assisted by medical practices that advised married women of childbearing age to be kept pregnant for optimal health (Soranus, *Gynecology* 1.11.42, arguing against the conventional wisdom). If not, their empty wombs made them unstable and less capable of subduing strong sexual desires (which could have been directed outside of marriage). The adolescent girl, often represented in the visual arts as part child, part woman on the brink of growing up, was domesticated by marriage (see Figures 28 and 29 in Chapter 2).

This rigid, hierarchical system did not allow for the self-possession and probity of middle-aged women. Matrons attained measures of legal and financial autonomy simply by outliving their fathers and husbands. Because most women entered marriages in which they remained under the control of their fathers (see Chapter 2), guardians were assigned to them to look after their financial interests upon their fathers' death. In reality, guardians rarely stood in their way. Marriages typically made between young women, barely older than girls, and men eight to ten years older ended up leaving widows behind. Those still able to have children remarried, often more than once, especially if they hailed from politically prominent families with influence to peddle. Mature women had to look after their own interests by default in this world in which death took away fathers and husbands in rapid succession. Marriages also could have been dissolved by divorce if sudden death did not part the couple. In extended periods of warfare with high casualty rates and social instability (in the republic, for example), matrons developed capacities for wielding authority within the family and community. Participation in religious rites, which linked households to the city, gave some matrons high visibility and social profiles (see Chapter 4).

Esteemed matrons could be depicted with masculine characteristics in literary and visual representations to demonstrate that only exceptional women could acquire the dignity, discipline, and high-mindedness of the male ideal. In the marble and painted portraits depicting the *grande dames* with flawless characters, features of middle or advanced age are emphasized, along with expressions of modest self-effacement or grim forbearance (see Figure 33 in Chapter 2 and Figure 65 in Chapter 3). Such women who modeled themselves on selective male qualities were striving upward, and their demeanors bore no negative implications about their sexuality (the commemorative portraits were likely to have been commissioned by their husbands and fathers, however). The trusted woman was defined as an honorary male.

The adoption of masculine traits by women could be seen as threatening and transgressive in other contexts. Mature women, cast as aggressive and domineering in invective, were mocked as sexually insatiable in graphic encounters in which their aging bodies only aroused disgust in their prospective lovers, the poet, and readers (Horace, *Epodes* 8 and 12). That they made sexual demands on their younger lovers was considered unbecoming and outrageous. Perhaps the vehemence of the attacks against active older women betrays resentment at their prominence and authority, if not their sexual antics. For women with more unorthodox appetites, the verdict was more severe and stereotypical. Women who desired women were depicted as unnaturally male in their appearance and behavior down to an enthusiasm for wrestling and drinking to excess – in fact, the caricature of the lesbian as a bodybuilder whose hardened muscles mimicked a virile physique has had a long life in Western popular culture (Martial, *Epigrams* 1.90, 7.67, 7.70). Lesbians were given Greek names in satire, as if to suggest that they were foreign or lowly slaves, and their sexual acts were seen as sordid and foul to the male poet. Representations of both honored and despised women were so highly conventionalized and rhetorical that we cannot accept them at face value, although it is striking that the adaptation of male practices ranged on a scale from the beneficial, elite regulation of the self (for society matrons) to base, predatory sex urges (for the no longer attractive dowagers and the subversive lesbians).

Yet the ennobling of the female with stellar masculine attributes succeeded brilliantly in the visual arts comprising imperial propaganda. First among these, the personification of the state assumed a heroically masculine demeanor in a female figure in official art and coinage. Roma, who stood for the concept of city and empire, was an armed female warrior (Figure 5). As a proper feminine noun in the gendered Latin language, Roma appears enthroned in a long garment or, more commonly, as a warrior outfitted with full gear in a short tunic, as we see here. Although poets refer to her as motherly in her protection of the city, she remains vigilant and militant in the style of a Roman general rather than that of a matron. The lineage of this figure includes the Greek goddess, Athena, who was frequently depicted with military gear, helmet, and shield. The bare breast, however, may strike us as a peculiar mode of dress for a warrior; yet, this motif came from the Amazons, the mythical enemies

5. Rome, Vatican Museums, Scala/Art Resource, N.Y., 80416. Frieze A of the Cancelleria Reliefs, 93–95 C.E., depicts the emperor Domitian going off to war, with Roma pushing him forward; she is the striding figure with the bare breast, helmet, and shield. Roma is shown here as a comrade in arms to the emperor, whose exploits are celebrated in the genre of the historical relief, sculptural panels decorating state monuments with imperial themes.

of the Greeks. According to myth, the Amazons removed one breast to enable them to fight better, yet in art they are depicted with both breasts, although often one is bare to signify their boldness, their exemption from the codes of conduct affecting women's lives. Romans drew on Greek culture as a resource, and the borrowing of the Amazon motif for the personification of Roma enhanced the woman warrior with the prestige of the Greek model and the power of the mythic enemies of Greece, now turned on those of Rome. A Roman citizen in the late republic, used to viewing Greek art that came to Rome first as war booty and then adopted as symbols of Rome's ascendancy, probably did not think of Roma as foreign nor exotic; rather, the personification became armed and dangerous in a perfectly acceptable manner, just as the upstanding and noble matrons gained stature for their emulation of masculine reserve and rigor.

The demarcation of gender was far from clear-cut. Rather than only manly men and demure women, a spectrum of gendered positions was available between the poles of extreme masculinity and femininity. Romans were, no doubt, better at spotting the relatives degrees of gender than we are and calculating the risks in adopting certain features. In visual depictions, especially in the portraits of individuals for which

Roman art is noted, gender is carefully and forcefully represented. Most portraits are obviously male or female to our eyes; yet, some images of children and adolescents resist easy identification as boys or girls. For example, a painted portrait placed on a mummy in Roman Egypt represents a beautiful child with enormous heavy-lidded, dark eyes and full, curving red lips (Figure 6). Most of us would assume that the subject is a girl because of the delicacy of the painted features; however, this is wrong. A contemporary viewer in Roman Egypt (see map) would recognize that the lock of hair behind the ear was worn by boys as part of a rite of initiation. In many cultures, the appearances of boys and girls could be confused until their features became more pronounced as masculine or feminine in adolescence; yet, the "feminine" looks of the painted portrait may have been preferred for elite boys in Roman Egypt. We should take this as a warning that we cannot always presume to know what gender looks like.

Gender and Status

The lot of Roman women was never universal. Within the boundaries of historical and regional developments, however, the most crucial factor in determining a woman's life was her social status, and for this, she depended on her father or husband if she were free born or her owner if she were enslaved (the emperor's top slaves amassed power and wealth, while, for the rest, the lot of slaves varied considerably depending on whether they worked in fields on agricultural estates or in workshops or townhouses in the city). In Roman society, status accrued through a system that organized the population in classes according to their birth and wealth. The classes are known as social orders and can be thought of as a pyramid with the peak representing the emperor and the rest of society fanning out below him in ranked gradations of importance. The highest order, the senatorial order, named for its membership in the governing council that ran the republic and then advised emperors, originally was a closed group of aristocratic families who possessed distinguished bloodlines and landed wealth. Beneath them was the equestrian

6. Berlin, Vorderasiatisches Museum, inv. 31161,4. Painted panel of a boy, from ca. 138–192 C.E., that decorated his mummy; although some think that the mummy portraits were painted from life, it may be that the artist improved his subject's looks or made them conform to cultural expectations.

order, consisting of men who served in administrative posts in Rome and abroad with their families; they also possessed a minimum income qualification. Farther down were the local elites who sat on town councils throughout the empire. The senators, equestrians, and local notables comprised the elite orders whose privileges and responsibilities revolved around public service, and their prominence in the political arena, either local or imperial, obligated them to uphold moral standards, although this stipulation was notoriously difficult to enforce.

The women of the elite orders maintained public profiles with appearances on state occasions at their husbands' side and, on their own, with the administration of cults, some of them part of the apparatus of state religion (see Chapter 4). Their prominence meant that their reputations needed to be spotless because any perceived lapse from the strict codes of conduct provided fodder for gossip and scandal that could damage their husbands. Although the house and family remained the traditional domain of women, even for the privileged wives of political leaders, some well-connected matrons participated at the edges of political life as partners of their husbands in state ceremony, as behind-the-scenes advisors, or as benefactors of their towns and patrons of citizens in need. These women's deeds were honored, as were their husbands', with marble statues erected on bases that were inscribed with their honors and titles; yet, the women were identified through their husbands' and fathers' names (the reverse situation rarely occurs, but see Plancia Magna). Because statues erected in the civic spaces of cities were among the highest honor granted to citizens, the erection of statues of women is a remarkable phenomenon. In early Rome, the statues of heroic women, such as Cloelia who led a group of women to safety from their Etruscan captors (fifth century B.C.E.), were put on pedestals in the forum, the civic center and main square. These heroines were not so much depicted as models for wives and mothers who could never aspire to these heroic feats but as examples from the distant past that could provide moral inspiration about Rome's destiny for men who were goaded to surpass the glory of mere women. Women who surpassed the limitations of the weaker sex in situations of impending political threat received the praise of their peers and honor from subsequent generations.

In the period of the empire, many more statues depicted women who led rather more humdrum lives. Honor was due to them because of their good deeds, made possible by their wealth and families' status. A pair of female statues erected in a portico in the agora (the main square) of Aphrodisias in Turkey (see map) may have depicted a mother and daughter or a pair of sisters in the early second century C.E. (Figures 7 and 8). Lacking bases with inscriptions, neither the subjects of the portrait statues nor their relationship to one another can be identified; yet, their location and expense suggests that they depicted women whose families comprised the city's ruling elite. Some art historians have detected signs of aging in the face of one figure (Figure 8), so tentatively they have identified the pair as mother and daughter. On close inspection, however,

7 and 8. Istanbul, Archaeological Museum, inv. 2268 and 2269; photos courtesy of
H.R. Goette. Statues of Women, probably dedicated as a pair in a portico in
Aphrodisias, Turkey, early second century C.E. Both statues display substantial
garments with cloaks enveloping the tunic-clad bodies in two different styles.
Although the clothing may have more to do with traditional statues types than with
fashionable attire, it enhances the modesty of the subjects by wrapping their figures
in yards of well-made cloth.

it is difficult to see the representation of age in the portrait faces, in part because of the damage done to them: that the heads had been broken off after the statues fell from their bases resulted in losses of the noses and chipping of the surfaces (as we see, the heads have since been reattached). It is interesting that both heads display the same hairstyle consisting of rows of high-piled curls forming a crest in the front while the rest of the hair is braided and gathered into a chignon in the back (seen under the veil worn over head in Figure 8) or a poneytail (Figure 7). This hairstyle, popularized by the women of the imperial court in the late first century C.E. (see Figure 88 in Chapter 4), may have been worn as part of the high-dress uniform by the pair of subjects in the eastern provinces (now Turkey), where images of the imperial women were seen on the reverses of coins or on the statues that crowded the city. If the husbands or fathers of the portrait subjects were equestrian officials, then their trips to Rome would have made them familiar with the modes of feminine adornment available in the capital (and the men were likely to have dedicated the statues as often noted in the inscriptions on extant statue bases). The images of a pair of elegantly turned-out women conferred honor on them and their families; rather than seeing the subjects only as fashionable (and frivolous) ladies, we can imagine the high hairstyles as crowning the stately presence and subdued demeanor of the portrait statues (see Chapter 3 on adornment).

Elites throughout the empire participated in a cosmopolitan culture with close ties to Rome despite the vast distances between some of the provinces and the capital. One such cosmopolitan, Herodes Atticus, built an ornate fountain in the Greek city of Olympia, site of the famous games, in the mid–second century C.E. (Figure 9). The basin wall was decorated with statues: those in the upper horizontal row depicted members of Herodes Atticus's family, while those below represented the emperor and his kin in Rome (focusing on Hadrian and the Antonine emperors and their wives). Women and children were included to demonstrate their importance in the continuation of the bloodlines and the future of the clans. More significantly, a comparison between two families, Herodes Atticus's and the imperial dynasty, is asserted visually

9. Reconstruction, British Museum publications, after S. Walker, *Greek and Roman Portraits*, fig. 12. Fountain of Herodes Atticus at the Sanctuary of Zeus in Olympia, Greece, ca. 150 C.E.; the basin wall is articulated in two stories with niches for statues framed by pairs of columns. This display wall was a popular architectural form in the second century C.E., especially in the Greek east, the part of the empire where Greek remained the language of choice and Hellenic culture was deeply entrenched. The Latin language and Roman culture had less appeal and affected mostly the elites in administrative posts.

through the arrangement of the statues. One may consider the family portrait gallery an act of overweening pride for a provincial, except that Herodes Atticus was a consummate politician both at home and abroad through his promotion of Hellenic culture in the Greek cities and his cultivation of emperors during his political posts in Rome. Herodes Atticus wielded influence both near and afar.

Elite women also promoted their families through public works projects and the manipulation of imagery. Plancia Magna funded the building of a new gate for her city, Perge in southwestern Turkey (see map) in the early second century C.E. (Figure 10). The gate also featured displays of statuary in niches along walls that represented members of Plancia Magna's family, the mythological founders of her city, and Roman emperors, such as Nerva, Trajan and his wife, Plotina, and Hadrian and his wife, Sabina. The cast of characters represented in the statues weaves together the past and present, Greek myth and Roman politics, but among the illustrious company of gods and heroes, the monument honors Plancia Magna's father and brother as city fathers. Despite the monument's emphasis on integrating local, Hellenic, and imperial figures, it is telling that women are represented in proportionally greater numbers in the statuary of the triple arch. Perhaps we should not be surprised that Plancia Magna dedicated the gate in her own name without a mention of her father or husband – in fact, the men are defined in relation to her as "father of Plancia Magna" and "brother of Plancia Magna." This unusual dedication of a woman on her own behalf makes sense in light of her illustrious career as priestess of various cults, a civic magistrate (offices open to women in the Greek east under Roman rule), and a benefactor graced with the title "daughter of the city." Furthermore, in her gift to her city, she transformed the defensive structure of a city gate into an impressive façade with a richly decorated courtyard that served as an anteroom for visitors to her city.

The elite social orders took up relatively little space near the top of the pyramid, and the widening base was reserved for the most numerous groups: citizens, residents without complete rights, freedmen, and slaves. Without honorary titles and political posts, the people composing the Roman masses were classified according to two criteria: their legal identities (as free born, freed slaves, or enslaved) and their wealth. The latter criterion may give us pause because this broad category consists of small shopkeepers, artisans, and laborers, including the down-and-out poor in the cities and the countryside. Most of these people lived from hand to mouth with little relief, except for the dole given out in cities. Yet there were entrepreneurial urbanites and prosperous farmers, many of whom profited from hard work and their ties to elites in a system in which the little man received favors and protection from a powerful patron. The patron, in turn, had a following of dependents, called clients, who could form an impressive entourage to the law courts or the forum and provide other services in promoting the patron's popularity or financial interests. This patronage system cut through rigid class lines to create bonds among individuals based on mutual self-interest.

The other criterion, that of legal identity, was equally important. The Roman economy was supported by slave labor. Under Roman law, slaves were defined as things (literally referred to as "speaking tools," in the legal code), and they were bought and sold as objects; furthermore, masters effectively had absolute powers of life and death over their slaves,

10. Fototeca Unione, Rome, neg. no. 22024. Gate of Plancia Magna, Perge, Turkey, ca. 120 C.E.; view of renovated gate with remains of arch; the gate was faced with two towers, beyond which was a horseshoe-shaped courtyard. A monumental triple arch faced the interior of the gate and closed the courtyard. Niches on both the courtyard walls and the triple arch contained statuary – some of the statue bases are inscribed in Greek, others in Latin. The walls were sheathed in marble.

and they could take possession of a slave's children. The condition of slaves varied from the miserable existence as field hands on big estates to the more comfortable life of maids in townhouses in the city who lived and worked closely with their mistresses. Yet the proximity to luxury and improved physical conditions did not often lessen the hostility and distrust inherent to the situation – the physician Galen was mortified that his mother bit her slave maids when she lost her temper (Galen, *Aff. Dig.* 8.1). Cruelty underwrote this system in which the threat of the whip held unruly or rebellious slaves in check. Unlike slaves in the American South, Roman slaves shared the skin color of their masters and some were well-educated to hold positions of responsibility in households or businesses as teachers or managers, for example. The stock character of the clever, ambitious slave, familiar in Roman comedy, embodies troubling aspects of the elite dependence on domestic slaves who were often represented as being more intelligent than their owners, possessing intimate knowledge of their masters' or mistresses' affairs and bodies, and requiring their trust to carry on their duties. Yet, this trust proved fragile because the slave never knew when blows would fall, and the owner never knew when humiliation was in store for being taken advantage of by a slave.

There was a future for Roman slaves who, once they were freed by their masters (many enterprising individuals bought their freedom from their masters by saving their pocket money), moved from nonentity to personhood. Most important, these freedmen and freedwomen became citizens, although with some restrictions of their rights (there were also ex-slaves with halfway status because they had been freed without legal formalities or in breach of certain restrictions). Masters freed slaves in their wills as rewards for their service; others freed them because they had careers in professions or businesses in which masters could invest (trade was considered a lowly activity unsuitable for aristocrats). In literary sources, freedmen and freedwomen were often depicted as the gatecrashers of polite society, vulgar folk who thought their money can buy them entry into the best circles, along with the accoutrements of the good life. Partly this attitude reflects the anxiety that a few ambitious freedmen aroused in elites rather than the reality of the humble freedman working in his shop with few prospects and even less interest in making a splash in society.

A relief depicting a man at work may demonstrate the conflicting desires and motivations of prosperous artisans and tradespeople, both freed and free born (Figure 11). It is assumed that the potter is a freedman although the relief lacks an inscription to inform us of his name and legal status (frequently the latter is not stated explicitly in inscriptions). Although we cannot identify the potter as a freedman with certainty, we can say the relief represents an urban social milieu in which freedmen and free born mixed. The couple sits facing each other, the man working while the woman, elaborately coifed and well-dressed, displays feminine

11. Richmond, Virginia Museum of Art, inv. 60.2. Relief of a potter and his wife, late first–early second centuries C.E. Most likely originally placed on the façade of the potter's tomb, the relief depicts the man glazing a cup while the woman holds objects, perhaps a palm fan and a small round bread, that refer to the domestic domain. Note the difference in chairs of the man and wife.

attributes as symbols of the wife's role (so we assume that they are a couple). Furthermore, her garment slips off her shoulder as an allusion to Venus, the goddess of female beauty and sexuality. Both this motif and the rigorously curled and plaited hairstyle suggest that the woman possesses the leisure to make herself attractive – it is significant that she is not depicted working, neither in the pottery workshop nor at her housework, mending or weaving. The composition of the relief with the pair seated opposite each another sets up a notion of equivalence, but the wife's appearance and demeanor assert that the potter is successful enough in his job to support such an elegant, idle creature. In reality, the wife was more likely to be fast at work most of the time, either at home or in the shop, but the relief projects the status to which the potter aspires (see Chapter 3).

The snobbery toward freedmen in the elite sources implies that a social distance should be kept from them. Yet, on the contrary, the relationship between patron (ex-master) and freedmen and freedwomen often was very close: some patrons and freedmen worked side by side in the same workshops, while others married their freedwomen. The marriages resulted from the control that masters had over their slaves' bodies: they could take sexual pleasure from their slaves, both male and female, who could not refuse their advances. The slave's plight is implicit in one of the founding stories of early Rome: Verginia, a free-born girl whose father was away on military service and was betrothed to be married, attracted the attention of the eminent Appius Claudius; Appius Claudius got an associate to declare under oath that she was his slave so that he could violate her without penalty, and the only way Verginia's father could save her honor was to kill her (Livy 3.44–48). This legendary tale of injustice to women and the powerless who could not prevail under the law exemplifies the lot of slave women – and, of course, the tragedy of the tale hangs on Verginia's inability to prove that she was *not* a slave. Other women, however, stood to gain from their relationships to masters who could free them in order to make them their wives. The freedwoman in this position experienced remarkable social advancement because not only did her master make her a citizen but the mistress of the house in which she formerly worked as a slave.

The rags-to-riches Cinderella stories were limited, however, because many of the freedwomen's husbands had modest means. According to the Augustan marriage laws (see Chapter 2), senators were not allowed to marry freedwomen, and it is likely that men who married their ex-slaves moved in social circles in which this would not cause comment. Marriages among equals, freedmen and freedwomen, offered them prerogatives that they lacked, even if they had lived as a couple while they were slaves. They then had rights over their children (if born after the mother was freed) and could pass on their property to their heirs. Freedmen celebrated their acquisition of families in the late republic and Augustan periods by proudly depicting their wives and children in funerary reliefs that graced their tombs. Yet the state of being a freedman lasted for only one generation because the freedman's children, were often citizens without the taint of slavery. Some prosperous freedmen and freedwomen looked to their sons to fulfill their ambitions by standing for public office, a prestigious avenue to elite status closed to freedmen. The prospects of social mobility, demonstrated by the slave's transformation into a citizen, were advanced further by the promise of children.

Wealthy freedmen could participate in the civic life of their towns by holding the office of *Augustales*, an honorary priesthood serving the cult of the emperor (the so-called imperial cult embraced a variety of activities). The *Augustales* enjoyed high visibility while officiating at various public ceremonies and festivals. More important was the requirement to invest their wealth in their community by sponsoring public works and donations. In these ways, they imitated elites and, no doubt, these responsibilities gratified their pride and sense of self-worth. A monument erected for one such priest was decorated with sculptural reliefs that evoke the career of the well-heeled freedman active in civic life (Figure 12). It is striking that the wife, the freedwoman Naevoleia Tyche, as dedicator, had her portrait placed above the inscription and put her name first in larger letters in the text. Her portrait stares out at the viewer through shutters, as is she has staged the proceedings below. The relief depicts a public benefaction, a grain distribution funded by the deceased (or, perhaps, by Naevoleia as part of the funerary observances for her husband). Families, with children of varying heights, are lined up to receive their portion of grain in an image that illustrates their dependence on the great man, C. Munatius Faustus. Another side of the monument depicts an official chair reserved for magistrates, a double-seater no less, a high honor granted to Munatius by the town counselors and, "by consensus of the people, on account of his merit," according to the inscription. The third side provides a relief depicting a merchant ship in full sail. Rather than a symbol of the passage of life, the ship may refer to Munatius's livelihood as a trader with seagoing vessels. The well-known account of the tomb of Trimalchio in the novel *Satyricon* by Petronius (also mid-first century C.E.) includes such biographical imagery as a ship to refer to the freedman's business savvy. The three reliefs depict the enterprise that earned Munatius his wealth (the ship), the generosity that brought him his standing in the town (the grain distribution), and the honors that accrued from this (the official chair). Evidently, Naevoleia had a stake in the prominent life that she commemorated and was highly motivated to erect this monument because Munatius had built a tomb for the couple, in which they were buried, in a different part of Pompeii. This monument, therefore, only served to display Munatius's glorious career. Are we not to think that the successes of Munatius owed at least something to the good graces of Naevoleia Tyche (Tyche means fortune) who looks over the scene? During her husband's lifetime, she was probably the good wife, supportive of her husband's ambitions and attentive to his needs, who stayed in the background. In the imagery of the monument she commissioned after his death, she casts herself as the presiding figure of fortune, who, after all, had ruled Munatius's life.

Republic and Empire

A few words about the historical development of Rome from republic to empire are in order, particularly in a book on social life and its institutions that ranges broadly over time and place. Both terms, republic and empire, refer to historical periods defined by political systems. At the traditional date of its founding, 753 B.C.E., Rome is often represented as an unimposing settlement of rustic folk; yet, recent excavations have shown that the city was built up with walls and opulent dwellings a century before (and the Sabines had been impressed by the urban amenities of the city; Livy 1.9.9–10). Impetus for cultural development has been found in Rome's neighbors, most notably the Etruscans, who had established a number of city-states in central Italy and ruled Rome from ca. 753–509 B.C.E., according to accounts of legendary foreign kings. Our knowledge of early Rome depends on later sources who color their stories with intimations of the promise of Rome's greatness; that is, the sources are not innocent nor without bias. It is more likely that the early

12. DAI, Rome, 77.2085. Relief from the funerary altar erected by Naevoleia Tyche for her husband, C. Munatius Faustus, and herself, as well as for their freed slaves, in Pompeii, mid–first century C.E. Relief panels decorated three sides of the altar.

cities of central Italy (Etruscan towns, Sabine settlements, and Rome included) had common cultural preferences drawn from the dominant powers of the Mediterranean basin, that is, from the Greeks and eastern peoples, as well as from the indigenous Italic cities closer to home. The stories Romans told about their origins reflect their need to define themselves against the Greeks, whose achievements had cast a long shadow, even without their colonies in southern Italy and Sicily. Roman notions about gender were sorted and shaped alongside those of the cultures that irrevocably influenced them.

The period of the republic, dating from ca. 509–31 B.C.E., witnessed
Rome's gradual growth from a city-state to an empire, an expansion
that strained the republic's political and social institutions with both
the rewards and responsibilities of its immense authority (see map). A
rigid and inflexible system of governance, along with a concentration of
political power in the hands of a few and the control of the military by
even fewer generals to whom the troops owed loyalty, ensured that the
transformation of Rome into a world capital was fraught with conflict
and violence. The ruling body of the senate, composed of aristocratic
male citizens, elected two co-executives called consuls annually as the
heads of state. Beneath the consuls, there was a ladder of administrative offices, filled by the election of leading male citizens who com-
peted for the prized posts. The highly competitive nature of republican
politics and its winner-take-all philosophy forced highly talented and
motivated leaders into opposition to the state: Julius Caesar's crossing
of the Rubicon in 49 B.C.E. represented one response to the intransi-
gency of the senate; his grandnephew, Octavian (later the first emperor,
Augustus), also used his army to pressure the senate early in his career in
43 B.C.E. The civil conflicts among the political class of the mid–first
century B.C.E. underscored not only elite power struggles but deep-
felt differences of opinion on how to govern the empire, on Rome's
role in the new world order. Running a vast land empire required sys-
tematic policies carried out by professional administrators, rather than
by greedy aristocrats or corrupt hired hands, as was more typically
the case.

Women emerge in the heroic tales of early Rome as forces of moral
authority, who frequently served as intermediaries among men (e.g.,
the Sabine women). Their actions, frequently involving self-sacrifice,
spurred their men to change political courses (recall the Sabine women
and Verginia above, and see Lucretia in Chapter 2). Women also organized themselves to act collectively. In the case of G. Marcius Coriolanus,
an exiled commander who marched on Rome in the early fifth century B.C.E., only the women of Rome effectively stopped his incursion
by appealing to Coriolanus's mother and wife to intervene. A mother

succeeded as an emissary for peace after the senate and priests had failed. This anecdote not only demonstrates the great respect that mothers commanded but elite women's conservative role in upholding the founding values and virtues of Rome, in which love of the land was entwined with love of kin and clan.

On occasion women took to the street to express themselves. Their participation in religion offered them experience in mobilizing their peers, organizing processions, and orchestrating public events for their cults (see Chapter 4). In 204 B.C.E. when the cult image of an important goddess was brought to Rome from Asia Minor (Turkey), a great state pageant was planned to receive the goddess by having the best Roman matrons line up to form a human chain to move the cult image from the port, Ostia, to Rome (see map). Quinta Claudia, a prominent woman, led the matrons; yet, in other versions of the tale, the barge carrying the cult image got stuck in mud, and it was up to Quinta Claudia to save the day (Figure 13). Claudia had been accused of being unchaste, and according to another source, her elegant clothes and hairstyle made her seem less than modest and pious. She prayed so that the goddess would allow her to release the barge if she was chaste; Claudia pulled the boat in − in a later version, she was a priestess, a Vestal Virgin, who towed the barge using her hair in place of rope − thus proving that she was chaste. Commemorated with a statue in the temple of the great mother, Quinta Claudia not only survived the attacks on her honor but became a heroine. The spectacle of matrons lining the road into the city and the celebrated test of virtue give a sense of the drama and pageantry of women's religious lives.

It is particularly interesting that women intervened on their own behalf when their own wealth was at stake. Women accumulated wealth through inheritance, dowries, and shrewd management of their money (and by working, if they were from the lower social orders); yet, rich women were seen as threats if their funds bought them freedom from social norms (see Chapter 2). The state had uses for women's gold in the early fourth century when the invading Gauls demanded ransom, and the good women of Rome contributed handsomely to the ransom payment. Yet, during the Punic War in 215 B.C.E., a sumptuary law, the *Lex Oppia*, forbade women to have more than half an ounce of gold, wear purple garments, or ride in horse-drawn carriages. When its repeal in 195 B.C.E. was threatened with failure, women took to the forum and streets to demonstrate their disapproval. The *Lex Oppia* aimed to restore women to their traditional modest and self-effacing roles in a period of crisis caused by military defeat. It was thought that a return to old-fashioned morality would appease the gods, who would then reverse the situation. Yet, at the time of the repeal in 195 B.C.E., the political and economic crisis had passed, and elite women were eager to resume their prerogatives. They were not pleased to hear of the speech of Cato, the moralizing spokesman for the old guard, in the senate:

> Let the women, then, be adorned not with gold nor precious stones, nor with bright-colored and purple clothing, but with modesty, with love of their husbands and children, with obedience, moderation, with the established laws, with our arms, our victories, and our trophies. (Zonaras 9.17)

It is striking that the passage of Cato's speech sets women's gold and precious stones against men's victories and trophies of war. A speaker in favor of the law's repeal states that "elegance of appearance, adornments and dress – these are the women's badges of honor, herein lie their delight and their glory, these are what our ancestors called the woman's world" (Livy 34.7.8–9, trans. W. Heinemann). To the conservatives like Cato, the law depriving rich women of luxurious status objects would keep them in control, while to others, feminine finery allowed women to participate in the competitive display of status in the republic. Their brilliant appearances, which served to distinguish them from women of the lower social orders (in contrast, recall Verginia's inability to convince the court that she was free born instead of a slave), complemented their husbands' and fathers' honorable careers. The women driving around the city in gilded carriages were, no doubt, the wives and mothers of senators, whose splendid vehicles drew attention to their families' nobility and

13. Rome, Capitoline Museums, inv. 321. Altar with relief panel depicting Quinta Claudia bringing in the cult image of the Great Mother, mid–first century C.E. Quinta Claudia may be represented in the form of the statue later erected in her honor in the goddess's temple – note the base beneath the figure.

income (that their use was regulated in the republic suggests that the sight of women on the move put some senators on edge; riding in carriages was later granted as a special privilege under Augustus in the empire; see Chapter 4). If drab matrons were accorded respect in public with passersby making way for them in the street, then these grand dames must have aroused the curiosity of bystanders, who strained to catch a glimpse of them in their shimmering purple tunics and gold jewelry. The spectacles that these women made of themselves were taken seriously because their appearances served to illustrate, or even justify, their privileges and to crystallize the wide gap between the lowest and highest social orders (see Chapter 3). At the most elite social levels, women's daily rounds – the protocols of arriving and departing at friends' homes – mimicked the magistrate's parade through the forum and to the law courts with his retinue of staff and servants carrying the insignia of office.

The period called the "empire" is usually seen to begin in the year 31 B.C.E. with Augustus becoming the head of the state. It lasts through most of the fifth century C.E. with Constantine moving the capital eastward to the city now known as Istanbul in 324 (see map) and with Romulus Augustulus (r. 475–6) as the last Roman emperor in the west. The first emperor, Augustus, who had emerged victorious from a bloody civil war unleashed by Julius Caesar's assassination in 44 B.C.E, focused on administrative reform to make an imperial bureaucracy capable of running the empire and on a visionary program to reform Roman society. The former plan brought in new men with the required skills for governance, yet the overall political agenda concentrated power in the hands of the emperor as an absolute ruler (although Augustus preferred the title of *princeps*, or "first citizen"). The program to reinvigorate the morality of the citizenry by encouraging marriage and childbirth through legislation was an altogether different matter; although it purported to revive traditional values, it brought private life, including the adultery of wives, under government scrutiny through laws that were difficult to enforce and very unpopular (see Chapter 2). Elite women, in particular, were targeted because of their alleged lack of compliance to the moral code. The so-called yoke of marriage was not only recommended but required to banish social problems, according to Augustus and his advisors. Even the imperial family was not above the reach of the law, as witnessed by Augustus ordering the exile of his daughter Julia for her flagrant violation of the adultery laws. However, his wife Livia achieved a unique position of distinction with considerable influence in public life that increased after Augustus's death in 14 C.E. (see Chapter 4).

Augustus also embarked on a program of urban renewal in Rome because the city, which had grown in a ramshackle fashion in the republic, was not fit as a world capital. The new monumental city center was provided with vast quantities of sculptural decoration, most of which illustrates themes that forge a continuity between Rome's past, its Augustan present, and its glorious future. The Ara Pacis, the altar of peace, erected

14. Alinari/Art Resource, New York, 99689. The Ara Pacis, Rome, 13–9 B.C.E., consists of an altar proper surrounded by a rectangular precinct of high walls decorated with relief panels; the long walls depict processions of priests, guards, and the imperial family – including women and children, see Figure 83 in Chapter 4; Tellus, the earth mother, is depicted on this relief panel from the precinct wall on the southeast side. Despite the delicate carving of the central figure, the discrepancy in size of the domestic animals below and the schematic composition of the flanking personifications of breezes lend the panel all the artistry of a policy paper in which each figure stands for another aspect of life improved by Augustus.

by the senate in honor of Augustus in 13–9 B.C.E., was decorated with scenes commemorating the dedication of the altar and setting the historical event in the heroic context of early Rome. One panel depicts a resplendent full-figured female with two babies on her ample lap (Figure 14). The theme of regeneration of the Roman populace and the natural world is writ large in the relief that represents the health and wellbeing of Rome: the human figures take center stage with the enthroned earth mother flanked by the personifications of breezes as indicated by their billowing drapery, while the stalks of grain refer to the thriving fields and the diminutive animals to the resiliency of the herds. It is characteristic that the fertile female body is equated with the land, now blooming forth without interruption due to the Augustan peace after the long hard years of war. In this example of state art, motherhood is idealized in Tellus, the figure with the handsome facial features of a goddess and whose cleavage and midriff are revealed through clinging and nearly transparent garments, an outfit that would bring scandal to a Roman matron. Clearly Tellus is a figure from the realm of art and, as such, would have been distinguished from a Roman matron by viewers; yet, the pure and rarefied version of femininity in this scene with its visual linking of babies and breasts, as well as the motherly lap cradling fruits of the field, plays into traditional ideas of womanhood. The political and patriotic aspects of Augustan themes appealed to many citizens throughout the empire who commissioned works of art and architecture in emulation of the famed Roman monuments for their own cities (Figure 15).

Augustus attempted to establish a dynasty in which his heirs would succeed him into office; yet, he had no son and his designated heirs did not survive him. This had to be a crushing blow to the man who fancied the imperial family as a model for society and who saw the dependence of the domestic and civic spheres as crucial to the state. Upon his death in 14 C.E., Tiberius, the son of Livia by her first marriage, became emperor. Subsequent emperors of the Julio-Claudian dynasty (Caligula, Claudius, Nero), named for both Augustus's relationship as Julius Caesar's grand-nephew and Livia's line, were descended from Augustus's granddaughter, great-granddaughter, and sister. After the demise of Nero, the last Julio-Claudian in 69 C.E., Vespasian gained control with the support of the army and founded Rome's second dynasty, the Flavians, with his two sons (Titus and Domitian) to follow him in office. In the second century C.E., however, a system of adoptive heirs was introduced in which the reigning emperor (Trajan, Hadrian) selected his successor from the elite corps of young men with the appropriate military and administrative backgrounds. The young Marcus Aurelius, favored by Hadrian who instructed *his* successor, Antoninus Pius, to adopt Marcus as the latter's heir, also married Antoninus's daughter to cement his relationship with the emperor. Even without dynastic motives, however, the marriage of

15. The Arch of the Sergii in Pula, Croatia, 2–20 c.e. Art Resource, N.Y. 17964. The arch was erected by a woman, Salvia Postuma Sergius, to commemorate three male relatives, one of whom served in a legion established by Augustus, while the other two were members of the local governing elite. Several features of the arch's ornament pay homage to the decoration of the Ara Pacis, which is striking considering the distance – both geographic and cultural – between this town on the Croatian coast and the city of Rome (see map).

the emperor's daughters and sisters was considered in light of the strategic possibilities of forging alliances with other prominent families.

In the late first century and early second century c.e., new blood was brought into the upper social orders, the senatorial and equestrian ranks. Many of these men were the local elites from outside of Italy, some from the Greek east. Already under Augustus, the senate was reduced in stature from a legislative body to an advisory council to the emperor; yet, admission to these orders represented the culmination of a career, especially for men from the provinces. Through these offices and honors, elite citizens from diverse regions participated in the politics of the empire and developed relationships with their far-flung peers so that they gradually had more in common with each another than with their subjects in their home towns. Their wives and daughters also became more cosmopolitan through this wider range of reference and occasional travel to the capital, which must have altered their perspectives and their sense of themselves.

The emperor affected the lives of citizens of the lower social orders through the handling of catastrophic events, wars, famine, and plague; yet, it is more difficult to see how imperial authority trickled down to the back streets of the great cities and the isolated villages of the empire. By the second century C.E., an emperor was thought to possess a superior ethical character and exert a paternal influence on his subjects. No emperor embodies this better than Trajan (98–117 C.E.), who distinguished himself as a superb commander in chief with his war in Dacia (Romania) and as an exemplary caretaker of the homeland. His social policies were particularly far-reaching beyond the usual free distributions of grain or money to which emperors resorted to maintain order in the cities. He enlarged and institutionalized a charitable system which benefited poor children in need of nourishment in the Italian towns and cities.

The importance of this program is evidenced in its depiction on a state monument, the Arch of Trajan at Benevento (in southern Italy, see map; Figure 16). The scene represents Trajan (now headless) in the left foreground holding a scroll, which probably listed the names of citizens eligible for support. Although all eyes are on Trajan, the center of the scene is a low table with food or sacks of money (the latter was distributed by officials). Two fathers are present, each leading a small child either toward or away from the table and carrying another on their shoulders. It is striking that there are no mothers present in the panel – the only female figures are four city goddesses, identified by their crenellated crowns

16. Alinari/Art Resource, New York, 16732. Scene of benefaction from the Arch of Trajan at Benevento, 114–118 C.E. This arch is covered in relief sculpture, panels depicting imperial policies at home and abroad, on both sides.

suggesting urban defenses, who indicate the scope of the program in the Italian cities. One city goddess holds a baby, but she does not function as a surrogate mother, rather the committee of fortified females reminds the viewer that that the program aimed to encourage reproduction among the lower social orders in order to provide Rome with manpower for the troops (boys were favored by the distribution). In the Ara Pacis panel (Figure 14), motherhood was respresented in nature that was, above all, productive, and the female body is on a par with agricultural yields and animal husbandry, elements of the domestic economy. In Trajan's Arch at Benevento, the urban and bureaucratic scene has suppressed motherhood and rewards fathers primarily for their sons, bred as potential soldiers. In both examples of state art, the female figures do not represent women, whether as individuals or representatives of their gender, but offer idealizations of the feminine that conform to the current ideology and meet the needs of the state.

In the following chapters, the images and voices of women are introduced in the form of works of art, archaeological artifacts, and inscriptions carved in stone (along with the occasional literary source) to explore
how they are represented or how they chose to represent themselves. In
some cases, the influence from state art and ideology predominates, while
in others, it merely serves as one standard that may or may not be heeded
(depending on a range of factors, including income, ambitions, and cultural or regional access to ideas and artists). Particular attention is paid
to the images of women whose lives were considered marginal and went
unnoticed by elites. Yet the officialdom of Rome remained a faraway
and disembodied entity to some of the empire's residents. Those who
lived in the rural hinterlands or frontier zones of the empire, or even citizens of the lower social orders in the cities, had less direct contact with
Roman authority. In some distant regions, life was relatively unaffected
by imperial rule because its bureaucracy was notably thin on the ground.
In others, the only official presence was the Roman army. Although by
definition a male institution, the army affected women because of its role
in acculturation, that is, by disseminating Roman values (along with the
Latin language) and granting citizenship upon discharge for auxiliaries
(legionaries received citizenship upon recruitment) (Figure 17). Women
traveled with the army despite rules against the soldier's marriages and
stood to gain much from marriage to a veteran with a sizeable pension
and means to buy land (see Chapter 3). Rome remained an urban civilization with its cities along the Mediterranean coast, yet tracts of the vast
interior were dotted with military roads and installations. Military forts
attracted trade and settlements that provided economic development and
cultural exchanges in which soldiers and citizens had to get on with each
other out of necessity.

Locals may have come to fear Roman soldiers for their patrols of
their communities. In territory already controlled by Roman forces the
patrols could turn violent quickly. In contested territory the troops were
known for their ruthless efficiency and stealth. The Column of Trajan,
erected in Rome in 113 C.E. to commemorate Trajan's conquest of Dacia
(Romania), depicts scenes of the army's work and life in a spiral frieze

17. Museo Archeologico, Florence. Bronze mask from Serre di Rapolano, first century C.E., that was worn as part of a helmet by the cavalry in parades and military exercises. That this mask appears feminine with its wavy locks parted in the center and its small features may allude to the mock battles performed for display. Some of these included Romans in Amazon masks to recreate legendary battles from the Greek past. It is curious to think of Roman horsemen playing the part of the heroic female warriors in reenactments of great mythological conflicts.

band (Figure 18). This particular scene depicts the aftermath of Roman victory with the destruction of the Dacian city, the walls of which are being dismantled by its own residents on Roman orders (in the left foreground). Behind them, families, women carrying babies and men leading children or heaving them onto their shoulders, are heading into forced exile from their land. Romans usually permitted the assimilation of foreigners (through military service, for example), except for defeated enemies who were usually slaughtered, if male, or taken as prisoners of war to be sold as slaves (some Dacians are rather nobly depicted poisoning themselves rather than being taken captive). The Roman sculptor identified the Dacian men by their grooming and costumes: the men wear long beards and trousers (a foreign costume to Roman men who wore togas), while the women have their heads wrapped with cloth. Their livestock trails after them as they become refugees and are forced off their land. The same subject is depicted in a relief panel from a victory monument erected by Trajan in Dacia (Figure 19). Here differences in style no doubt reflect the audiences for the two monuments: a metropolitan Roman public eager for images of the army in action, and the people of the recently conquered territory who experienced the fighting and its aftermath. In both monuments, the Dacians typically appear with women and children when they are defeated, as if their possession of families made them even more vulnerable and their loss of country and home all the more poignant. This point of view conforms to Roman

18. Panel LV–LVI, LXXV–LXXVI, Alinari/Art Resource, N.Y., 179645. The Column of Trajan, Rome, 113 c.e., was erected in the Forum of Trajan in a piazza between the Latin and Greek libraries, a fitting location for the spiral frieze that was based on Trajan's written commentary on his campaigns, now lost. Many of the scenes depict the Roman army's preparations for fighting, building camps, clearing forests, and sacrificing to their gods.

19. DAI, Rome, 69.3285. Trophy of Trajan, Adamklissi, metope XLII, depicting a Dacian family fleeing in an oxcart as refugees, 109 C.E. Note the difference in the style between this relief and the one from the Column of Trajan in Rome: local sculptors carved the reliefs on the Troply at Adamklissi, and the flattened and simplified forms may have appealed to its audience.

ideas about the discipline of the fighting force since they saw wives and children as liabilities for their own soldiers. It is characteristic that the Romans projected their own values, their sense of pride and honor, on their enemy who, after all, was attempting to defend country and kin. The need to preserve the family, as the basic unit of social organization and moral authority, was a paramount concern of Romans, and it is to marriage and the family to which we turn.

CHAPTER 2

MARRIAGE AND THE

FAMILY

From their teens through middle or later life, free Roman women were married and gained respectability as *matronae*, a category that specifically denoted their marital state and the motherhood that accompanied it because children were the goal of marriage. From childhood and adolescence girls looked to marriage as the threshold of adulthood, even though elite girls may have been married early in their teens, while most other brides were young women in their late teens or early twenties. If a woman remained wedded to one man, she was celebrated as the *univira* (literally, the one-man woman), devoted to her husband. Reality impinged on this ideal because the custom of women marrying men about ten years older made many matrons widows, and divorce dissolved infelicitous or unproductive unions easily without a stigma. Remarriage was an option for the widow or divorcée from an aristocratic family who was still in her childbearing years, and, in fact, the frequency of remarriage in elite circles was high. When we speak of Roman girls as having irrevocable futures as married women, we should recall that the Roman institution of marriage provided a variety of experiences for women throughout the course of a life and was defined by custom and the families involved rather than by legal stipulations.

Roman law simply stated that a union was established if the couple intended it to be so, and they could express their intent by living together as man and wife (they should also possess the legal capacity to marry, *conubium*). In the early republic, there were two forms of marriage, one with *manus* (literally hand) and one without. Marriage with *manus* entailed the bride's coming under the authority of her husband (of her father-in-law if still living) as if she was a minor in his care; marriage without *manus*, which became the norm by the first century B.C.E., indicated that the wife stayed under the legal jurisdiction of her own father, inherited from him, and lived with her husband but without becoming part of his family, which was defined by relationships of the male line. The role of wives as intermediaries between families may derive from deep-seated Roman convictions about marriage as recounted in founding myths, such as the Rape of the Sabine Women.

Moralizing Exempla

For women, marriage was a vocation, for men a duty. In the rhetoric of marriage, a strain of misogyny emerges that casts younger women as vain, deceptive, and uncontrollable creatures. As marriage is necessary to produce and raise legitimate offspring, women must be endured:

> If we could get on without a wife, Romans, we would all avoid that annoyance; but since nature has ordained that we can neither live very comfortably with them nor at all without them, we must take thought for our lasting well-being rather than for the pleasure of the moment. (Gellius, *Attic Nights*, 1.6.2, trans. S. Dixon)

Q. Caecilius Metellus Numidicus, censor in 102 B.C.E., said this in a speech about the benefits of marriage, of which the only one worth crowing about was the begetting of heirs as citizens, and soldiers. In fact, an early divorce resulted from a wife's inability to bear children: in 230 B.C.E. Sp. Carvilius Ruga told the censors that he loved his wife, but his marriage had not served the purposes of procreation. Ruga's peers did not approve of his action, possibly because early Roman law only permitted divorce if the wife committed adultery, poisoned children, or substituted the keys (indicating that wives were pilfering household supplies or were drinking wine on the sly). By divorcing a decent woman, Ruga had to make amends by returning her dowry (the husband kept the dowry if the wife committed the above crimes). In Ruga's time, a wife still could be considered "blameless."

The rhetoric of misogyny flourished in the Roman empire although its effect on real life, relationships between men and women, social customs and institutions was rather complex. Rhetoric was a literary form with its own conventions and set pieces that did not reflect reality nor dictate behavior; rhetoric also informed social satire, which often featured a gallery of female stereotypes, such as the domineering wife, the busybody, the spendthrift, and the sexually insatiable crone, among others. In the early second century C.E., the poet Juvenal wrote his sixth Satire, long considered the bible of invective against women; yet, its target is adulterous wives and, by extension, marriage. Juvenal begins by lamenting that the virtue of pudicitia (chastity for married women) is on the wane and recounts a number and variety of faithless wives, from women sleeping with lowly actors and gladiators to Messalina (wife of Claudius; see Chapter 4) described bluntly as a *meretrix Augusta*, the imperial woman as whore, and on to other feminine foibles symptomatic of adultery, such as gossip, intellectual pretensions (as exhibited by the learned woman, the *matrona docta*), and vanity. The comedies of the republican stage offered another female stereotype in the form of the shrewd wife who outmaneuvers her philandering husband by tricking him with the help of the slaves (see, for example, Plautus, *Casina*).

> "There is nothing that a woman will not permit herself to do, nothing that she deems shameful, when she encircles her neck with green emeralds, and fastens huge pearls to her elongated ears; there is nothing more intolerable than a wealthy woman. Meanwhile she ridiculously puffs out and disfigures her face with lumps of dough; she reeks of rich cosmetics which stick to the lips of her unfortunate husband. Her lover she will meet with clean-washed skin; but when does she ever care to look nice at home? (Juvenal, *Satire* 6. 457–465, trans. P. Green)

The jewels and makeup may seem innocent enough to the modern consumer, but to the satirist, they summoned the dangers of wealth and leisure, the former allowing the wife freedom to do as she pleased (and to lord over her husband), while the latter brings about corruption through the draining away of a fortune by frivolous expenditures and the immorality of an extramarital affair. Juvenal describes the off-putting sight of a mature woman trying to appear beautiful: the earlobes stretched under the weight of the oversized earrings, the pasty makeup, and smelly creams. The matron's beauty regimen produced quite the opposite of its intended effects, and her efforts suggested the fraudulent nature of her adulterous adventure. The long-suffering husband only saw his wife at her disgusting toilette but never glimpsed the final transformation with its so-called natural-looking radiance, which was for the lover's eyes only.

Why the obsession with adultery? The objective of Roman marriage to bear legitimate heirs raised concerns in this regard, but we should also look to the larger issue of the family and its management. *Familia* is a legal term that defined the mother, children, and slaves, and in other contexts, indicated only the household's slaves. Many Roman households conformed, more or less, to our notion of the nuclear family of parents and children, but the inclusion of slaves in the terminology of *familia* suggests the importance of the family's common property. As a vehicle for the transmission of property through the generations, the elite family needed to regulate its membership and oversee its affairs, its wealth held in landed estates and its other financial interests. By tradition and law, the *paterfamilias* (the father) ruled the household and had *patria potestas*, the right of life and death over his dependents. Although this right was tempered by social pressure – fathers did not routinely nor even rarely kill their sons or daughters in early Rome – we should see this as an expression of the immense authority of the *paterfamilias*, who also convened family councils to consider the selection of spouses for his children, to force married offspring to divorce if necessary, and to punish wayward behavior, the most serious being that which dishonored the family. Adultery was among the crimes that brought shame and, therefore, merited the most serious punishment.

The double standard operated with full force because adultery was a crime on the part of women but not necessarily for men. Elite men could always take their pleasure with slave girls, market women, actresses, or other lowly women considered *infamis*, that is disreputable and beneath the attention of the law. As long as a husband avoided respectable women as sexual partners and did not demean himself in acts considered unmanly (e.g., the passive role in homosexual coupling), his extramarital activities were not worth mentioning. The *matrona* had no leeway – any sexual liaison outside of marriage was forbidden, although aristocratic women's alleged tastes for gladiators or other lowlife types obsessed moralists and

20. From France but in New York, Metropolitan Museum of Art, inv. 81.10.245. Glass cup with scenes of gladiators in relief, 50–80 C.E. Kitchenware reflects popular culture and, in this case, the fascination with the gladiator. The heroics of the amphitheater may have been mixed with an erotic charge, given the gladiator's appeal to women.

satirists, such as Juvenal in *Satire Six* (Figure 20). The family councils that dealt with cheating wives were evidently not rigorous enough for Augustus, who instituted laws that made adultery a public crime to be tried in a court of law.

Moral Reform

Augustus's Julian laws on marriage and adultery of 18 B.C.E. and 9 C.E. prescribed the measures a husband had to take when he discovered his wife's betrayal (if not, he could be held liable for "pimping" for her). He must divorce her immediately; if he had caught his wife and her lover in the act, he could kill the lover under certain conditions. The lover's trial proceeded first, and, if found guilty, the wife would then be tried. The convicted pair could suffer exile to separate islands and the loss of property; furthermore, adulteresses could not remarry free-born Romans after the period of exile. These procedures took the affairs of the bedroom into the public domain of the forum in an unprecedented attempt at moral reform that, despite its lack of success, announced the sweeping mission of the new regime to impose higher standards of behavior, responsibility, and sanctity on elite citizens who had indulged themselves too long (for the permissive society of the late republic, see the section "Mistresses and Love Poetry"). It was as if Augustus acted as the *paterfamilias patriae*, the father of his country, because he could not trust his citizens to take control of their wives (thus, the law compelled injured husbands to denounce them). What was once an offense against a man's honor became a crime against the institution of marriage and the state. Not confined solely to a preoccupation of Augustus, the Julian laws were also reinstated by the emperor Domitian in the 90s C.E.

21. Rome, Vatican Museums, Museo Chiaramonti, inv. 2109, Alinari/Art Resource, N.Y., 114679. Relief of Lucius Vibius Felix, 13 B.C.E.–5 C.E., depicts a family group. According to the inscription below the image, the father is free born, the mother is a freedwoman (of a woman, but her name Vecilia Hilara is cut off on the panel's right edge), and the son's legal status is not explicity stated (*CIL* 6.28774). That the son is represented as a portrait bust rather than a half-figure may indicate that he died early in life.

Not only directed at those who polluted the sacred state of matrimony, the Julian laws also provided incentives to marry and bear children, and penalized those who remained single and childless. Well-off men who were avoiding marriage forfeited some rights to inherit estates and legacies. Free-born women who had three children, and freedwomen who had four, were exempt from the requirements of having a guardian; that is, they could freely dispose of property and make wills without securing permission. The laws also stipulated that free-born men, except senators, could marry freedwomen. The marriage laws reflected a concern with the birth rate and the need to produce more Romans as citizen-soldiers, and they also acknowledged the fragility of life in a world in which a child's reaching adulthood was never taken for granted (see discussion on demographics). Freedwomen could also benefit by marrying above their station (usually, their former masters), and it is telling that only the highest order, the senatorial, was restricted from their list of suitable mates. The Julian laws, therefore, suggest Augustus's attempts at social engineering by reinforcing status distinctions and their privileges, while, at the same time, allowing some upward mobility as a reward for compliance (Figure 21). The onus, however, fell on the equestrian and senatorial orders who were perceived as leading extravagant, profligate lives with little regard for the models of their noble forbears. That the legislation took its toll is suggested by the following anecdote about a public protest against the restrictions imposed by Augustus:

> When the equestrians . . . persistently called for its (*the Julian laws*) repeal at a public show, he (Augustus) sent for the children of Germanicus (Livia's grandson) and exhibited them, some in his own lap and some in their father's, intimating by his gestures and expression that they should not refuse to follow that young man's example. (Suetonius, *Augustus* 34.2, trans. R. Graves).

The extreme measures imposed by the Julian laws met with an equally brazen reaction, which took place in the theater. The theater and amphitheater were places in which citizens could cheer or boo the emperor without fear of repercussions because of the anonymity of the crowd, but equestrians and senators may have been identified because they were seated according to their rank. It is striking that Augustus chose to display the progeny of his family (or, rather, that of his wife, Livia), given his own difficulty in controlling his free-spirited daughter Julia, who was exiled for her promiscuity and shameless flaunting of the moral legislation in 2 C.E. For the emperor's daughter, as with other scions of aristocratic families, the charges of immorality may have masked political motivations (see Chapter 4). Yet Julia was not alone in her wild carousing; she exemplified the way of life for a set of young, wealthy, and bored socialites who thumbed their noses at the polite society of their elders. Traces of this world of gilded youth, their feverish self-preoccupation and never-ending parties, are found in poetry of the late first century B.C.E.

Mistresses and Love Poetry

The poetry of Catullus (84–54 B.C.E.) and Propertius (before 57 B.C.E., between 16 B.C.E. and 2 C.E.), for example, offers glimpses of love affairs between single young men-about-town (the narrators) and the objects of their desire, married women or those living independently (as courtesans or actresses). Of course, the poems did not document the poets' love lives in the manner of the tabloid press but, rather, suggest how a group of young intellectuals imagined a heady, volatile world of romantic trysts and emotional crises, and filtered the scenarios of desire through Greek literary forms. The illicit relationships and extramarital sex flew in the face of traditional morality in the late republic (pre-Augustan reforms), and this defiance was one of the points of the exercise. There was one young woman, Sulpicia, writing love poems in this period, but the masculine voice of the genre prevails because only a few of her poems remain (for the voice of a girl in love, see later). The lovers are at the beck and call of their women in the elegies, which often cast the male narrator as "enslaved" to his mistress, as if mocking the vocabulary of the forum and law courts. Living independently – even if married – and only concerned with their own pleasure, the women of the poems appear to be elegant and fashionable in both the society banquets and the *demimonde*, the taverns and back alleys of Rome. They exhibit no matronly qualities and, in fact, seem downright masculine in their pursuit of sexual partners and in their cold-eyed way of breaking off the affairs. In fact, the lifestyle of the courtesan required the attention of many lovers for its maintenance, for the gifts that fed and clothed her. To the needy and impoverished poet, she is unfaithful and greedy. Scholarship has blurred the lines of reality and fiction in the works of Catullus because his mistress has been identified as a historical figure: Clodia, a mature married woman of an extremely illustrious family who took on another younger lover after her illicit affair with the poet (although only tentative, the identification has become as familiar as fact in the scholarship). We should recognize that the poets' mistresses were constructions rather than historical personalities and, although fictional, these imperious characters have some bearing on perceptions of steely, self-willed women. Catullus charts the rise and fall of passion in a series of elegies that resound initially with joy and then despair as the affair wanes. Here is a poem that declares the lovers' intention to seize the moment (and flout social conventions) at the beginning of the affair:

> "Let us live and love, my Lesbia. Here's
> a copper coin for the criticism
> of elderly men with exalted morals.
> Suns have the power to set and return.
> Our light is brief and once it fails,
> we have to sleep in the dark forever.
> Give me a thousand kisses, a hundred,
> another thousand, a second hundred,
> a thousand again, a hundred more
> until we ourselves lose track of the score,
> confusing the kissing count as a sly
> method of thwarting the evil eye."
>
> (Catullus 5, trans. D. Mulroy)

This freewheeling society gathered in dinner parties in the fine town-houses in which the city's fathers mingled with the poets' bohemian set who sought out loaded tables and full cups of wine. In a speech defending a young man's character against the depravity of Clodia (*Pro Caelio* 35), Cicero lists the other amusements of this set, besides love affairs and orgies: beach parties, carousing, singing, musical entertainments, pleasure boats and gardens. Propertius, like Catullus, turned away from military and political themes: "Let somebody else better suited tell of the Parthian troubles, how they dragged their feet to the truce to return the standards they took from Crassus and how, if Augustus does not subdue them, it will be to leave his sons the job and its glory. . . . Meanwhile, I pass the evenings drinking and singing songs until I can see the sunbeams dance in my glass" (Propertius 4.6.85–102, trans. D. Slavitt; in 20 B.C.E. Augustus had negotiated the return of military standards from the Parthians, who had captured them from the general Crassus in 53 B.C.E.). For poets, rounds of parties, rather than careers of political offices or military honors, gave sustenance, and if they lifted their glasses to Augustus, it was out of relief that the upheaval of the civil wars of the thirties B.C.E. was over.

During the dinner party, various social types engaged in lively banter and amorous encounters; the grand dames, kept mistresses, and actresses, along with the husbands, literary types, and unattached young men mixed together in this cultural institution. Even when reclining with her husband, a woman was not safe from the advances of an admirer: Ovid suggests that a lover send signals with discreet glances, nods, and the brushing of feet (*Amores* 1.4.1–4, 15–18). Although the dinner party proceeded by a set of rules that determined seating and the host's program of conversational topics or entertainment, propriety may have lapsed with the flow of the wine as the evening wore on (Figure 22). Banquets both broke down and reinforced social barriers; yet, their risqué reputations also were enhanced in literary accounts, set pieces for so-called Roman decadence. In reality, many banquets may have been rather staid affairs with little or no improvised entertainment or even the spontaneous "acting out" of besotted guests. As banquets provided occasions for the political class to socialize outside of the forum, the conversations turned to the business

22. Naples, Museo Archeologico Nazionale from Pompeii. Scala/Art Resource
N.Y., 173889. Wall painting from the House of the Chaste Lovers, IX, 12, 6–7, first
century C.E., with scenes of couples reclining at a banquet. The female participants
look like the professional women, *hetairai*, of Greek symposia. Although allusions to
Hellenic culture are common in Pompeii, the room adorned by the paintings was
part of a commercial establishment, not usually the sort of place adorned with motifs
of high culture.

of the day and, no doubt, alliances were forged and deals were made in
these convivial encounters. In this clubhouse atmosphere of male bond-
ing and one-upmanship among the elite, wives and mistresses mingled –
it would be interesting to know how they sized each other up; if they saw
each other as anything more than the competition for the favors of their
husbands or paramours. The statesmen Cicero tells of being shocked by
the presence of Cytheris, a notorious actress, at one such party (*Letters to
his friends*, 9.26.1–2), but we have no responses from outraged, bemused,
or indifferent matrons to the professional women.

The introduction of women as guests into the *triclinium*, the dining room, derived from Etruscan traditions. Greek men dined with their male guests, and enjoyed a female presence in the form of entertainers, dancers, or prostitutes. Etruscans were noted in antiquity for their lavish and unencumbered lifestyle in which men and women sat together not only at meals but also at games; to Greek eyes, Etruscan women's freedom of movement and sumptuous attire indicated their rampant sexuality (Figure 23). Some modern scholars have attributed the prominence of women in Etruscan art and culture to a matriarchal society; however, this cannot be supported despite the visibility and wealth of

23. From Vulci, in Boston, Museum of Fine Arts, 86.145. Lid of a marble sarcophagus, mid–fourth century B.C.E., depicting a married couple, Larth Tetnies and Thanchvil Tarnai, embracing in bed under a blanket, a symbol of their marriage. The impassive faces are a convention of Greek art, but the tender embrace with hands caressing necks and backs is characteristic of the expressive effects of Etruscan art.

women. Although scholars have tended to see archaic Rome as falling under Etruscan influence, it is more likely that the cultures of the early Italian cities had many features in common from the Greek, eastern, and Italic civilizations that dominated their world. The Etruscans were no more to blame for Roman lifestyles than their other Mediterranean neighbors.

Honor and Shame

In the history of early Rome as recounted by Livy, the encounters between Etruscan rulers and Roman matrons prove to be catalysts for political revolt and renewal (Livy 1.57–60). The story of Lucretia is telling in this regard because it pivots on a contest of wifely virtue that began in a drinking party. The son of the Etruscan king and other officers bragged about their wives' characters in a session in their tent during a lull in a campaign, and they decided to ride home to check on how their women were spending their time alone. The Etruscan princesses were found to be amusing themselves at an elaborate feast, while Lucretia was spinning wool with her staff late into the night. Smitten by her virtue and her beauty, the Etruscan prince returned to Lucretia's house a few days later determined to have his way with her. After his words had no effect, he threatened to slay her and his slave, claiming that he had found them together in bed. Lucretia submitted to him, summoned her father and husband the next day to inform them of what happened, and stabbed herself to death once they promise to avenge her. As a consequence of this crime, the Etruscan kings were ousted from Rome and the republic was founded in 509 B.C.E.

As in the legend of the Sabine women, the story of Lucretia exemplified personal honor and public dignity on the part of its heroine in the face of the most base and vile of crimes perpetuated by her aggressor. In both tales, the rapes led to the establishment of new communities or regimes in which the balance of power was recalibrated or, at least, reconciled to the needs of the interested parties. As matrons who sacrificed themselves to the greater good of Rome, the Sabine women and

Lucretia became models of female heroism whose actions affected the political order. For better or worse, the Roman discourse on marriage cast the bride as an instrument of exchange and every matron as a potential source for scandal – after all, it was both Lucretia's virtuous woolwork and her beauty that aroused the Etruscan prince.

Passages and Protocols

Roman girls grew up on the stories of captured brides and ravished matrons, but their own lives were far more sheltered if they came from elite families precarious if they came from the lower social orders. They spent their childhood in their fathers' households, some of them occupying special places as the treasured little girl, playing and learning the skills required of them as adults, while most of the others had begun to work at early ages to help support their family or their master, if they were slaves. Ancient sources tend to be sentimental about the lives of Roman girls, especially if they had elite fathers to mourn their premature deaths or trumpet their promising marriages, the moments when girls emerge in the texts, the epitaphs, or letters. Education for girls was an informal affair emphasizing domestic skills, with reading and writing beyond an elementary level of literacy only taught to daughters of wealthy or aristocratic families who could afford such a luxury (girls also may have sat in on their brothers' lessons). Verginia, the daughter of a soldier in early Rome, was being escorted to school when she was taken into custody unfairly, but her education did not serve to distinguish her from the slave that her captor insisted she was (Livy 3.44.4 and Dion. Hal. 11.28.3; see Chapter 1, also on the education of some slaves).

Among the tasks of household management, woolwork figures prominently in rhetoric and archaeology. The woman spinning wool or weaving at her loom connoted the traditional virtues of industry, thrift, and chastity, above all (to moralists, housewives exhausted by endless hours of such manual labor could be relied upon to stay out of trouble). Many tombstones simply evoke the worthy matron's

24. New York, Metropolitan Museum of Art, inv. 37.129a–b. A marble ash urn in the shape of a wool basket was a fitting final resting place for a matron whose virtue was summoned by her workbasket, now her tomb. It dates to the first or second centuries C.E.

qualities by stating *"lanam fecit,"* she made wool (Figure 24). Skill in weaving summoned the ideal of the old-fashioned wife, an ideal still so highly desirable in the imperial period that sophisticated, cosseted women had to flaunt their abilities in making garments even though it was highly unlikely that they ever labored over the loom or even directly supervised their staff: Suetonius recounts that the women of Augustus's family (his wife Livia, sister Octavia, daughter Julia, etc.,) made Augustus's togas and tunics, surely a statement in which ideology mastered reality (Suetonius, *Augustus*, 73). Compare the current snobbery about gourmet food and its time-consuming preparation that appeals to certain rarefied notions of tradition and domesticity, which can only be afforded by the affluent. Wool was featured in rituals of venerable antiquity: uncombed wool was wound on the doorways of the husband's house to welcome the bride, so deeply ingrained was the ideal of the spindle with the bride's role in increasing the wealth of her husband's house. Woolworking equipment, such as loomweights, spindles, and distaffs, have been found in large numbers in the houses of Pompeii and other sites (see Chapter 3), and we should imagine girls playing around the atrium court in which the matron supervised her maids at their looms. Models of domestic diligence were always before the girls, whose adolescence was brief given the relatively early ages of marriage.

Girls played with dolls, of course (Figure 25). Some of the dolls, made of ivory or bone (rag dolls have not survived as well as the more luxurious versions), had the bodies of adult women with rounded breasts and swelling hips with joints at shoulders and hips; some also bend at the elbows and knees. The hair is frequently fashioned in the styles worn by the current imperial women, as seen in the tower made of wound braids,

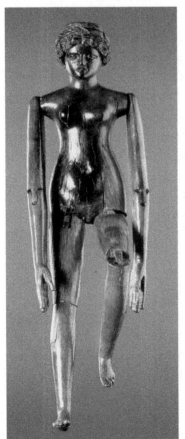

25. Capitoline Museums, Rome. Ivory jointed doll found in the sarcophagus of Crepereia Tryphaena, mid-second century C.E. The "mobility" of the doll with jointed limbs differs from works of sculpture, although we should probably think of sculptures "in motion," that is, carried in processions on festival days. Note the mature body type with breasts and hips that would have been clothed with her own wardrobe. Dolls were said to have been given up on girls' wedding days, but here the doll was laid in the tomb for the girl who died before her time.

which recalls the coiffures of the elder Faustina, wife of the emperor Antoninus Pius (r. 138–161 c.e.). Rather than being cradled in girls' arms, this doll was guided into moving and seated poses in imitation of a matron's various postures and, once decently clothed, could have provided its owner valuable practice in getting through the day's routine with the proper comportment and poise (note that the draped mantle may have been awkward to manage in some circumstances and the length of the tunic or stola, especially if made of wool, would have been restrictive as well). The repertory of gestures, carriage, and demeanor, what we call body language, mattered because a matron not only had to look her part but she had to carry herself with modesty and dignity at all times. This required practice early on with the miniature adult bodies of their dolls.

In their play with dolls, girls may have restaged the daily dramas of the household through an imagined adult persona. Their playmates may have included not only their siblings but the slave children as well. In elite households, slave minders took care of the children while the mother managed household affairs. Slave women had children of their own who formed part of the household until they were made useful and set to household tasks. In the confines of the domus, the social orders mixed as children played and the materfamilias supervised her staff. While darting in and out of the atrium during their games, girls had ample opportunity to see how their mother ran the household, to mimic her in ordering their siblings or the slave children about (or vice versa in the inversion of social roles?).

Puellae Doctae

Some elite girls received a literary education beyond the basics of reading and writing. This instruction was not provided to prepare them for occupations (for an exception, see Hermione Grammatike in Chapter 3); rather, it made certain well-bred girls better companions for their husbands, who were about eight to ten years older and practiced law or held offices, careers that required oratorical skills and speechwriting. Evidence of the talents of learned girls emerged when they marry. The

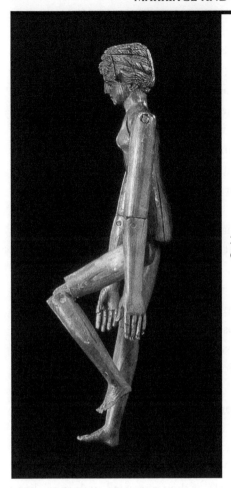

26. Profile view of ivory doll of
Crepercia Tryphaena (see Fig. 25).

younger Pliny (ca. 61–112 C.E.) praises his third wife Calpurnia: "She
is highly intelligent and a careful housewife, and her devotion to me is
a sure indication of her virtue. In addition, this love has given her an
interest in literature: she keeps copies of my works to read again and
again and even learn by heart.... She has even set my verses to music
and sings them, to the accompaniment of her lyre, with no musician to
teach her but the best of masters, love" (Pliny, *Epistles*, 4.19. trans. B.
Radice). Pliny and his young bride move in the most exclusive society,
given his status as an advisor to emperors such as Trajan. Some aristocratic families traditionally educated their daughters as a matter of pride,

perhaps as an additional credential to further distinguish themselves from those below them in the pecking order by indulging in luxuries (see the biography of Cornelia, for example, in Chapter 4) and included in their studies the liberal arts and performing arts, such as literature and music. Note that Pliny claims his wife's literary interests stem from her desire to please him rather than from intellectual curiosity, but we do not have her explanation of her motivation; it is impossible to know whether she was truly Pliny's biggest fan or simply lacked another outlet for her intelligence.

A funerary stele from the Roman colony at Mérida, Spain, represents a girl holding a stringed instrument similar to a guitar or lute (Figure 27). With fingers plucking the strings, the figure of Lutatia Lupata is commemorated in the act of making music, which was a pastime of aristocratic women, such as Calpurnia. Yet the inscription on the stele identifies Lutatia Lupata as the foster-daughter of Lutatia Severa, who dedicated the stele. Both Lutatias were provincials from the lower social orders whose world differed drastically from that of Pliny and his young bride in Rome.

The musical instrument may provide the key to clarify the relationships here. The lute may represent an occupation by evoking the musical talents of women who entertained for a living in taverns or private parties as courtesans or prostitutes. The professional women earned more, or appealed to more affluent clientele, if they possessed such specialized skills or even cultivated an air of gentility. Lutatia Lupata could have been both an apprentice and foster-child to Lutatia Severa, who mourned the loss of her protégé and colleague-in-training. That Severa served to profit from Lupata's skills by collecting her future fees did not necessarily rule out her genuine grief at the girl's premature death. The terse epitaph typically does not offer emotional declarations nor biography but Lupata may have been a slave, who was freed by Severa and then lived in her care in a relationship of quasi-adoption (that Lupata was an abandoned infant taken in by Severa reflects stereotypical notions about *alumnae* or foster-children not borne out by the evidence). Children were expected to help support their families and later their elderly parents in all but the

27. Mérida, National Museum of Roman Art. The stele of Lutatia Lupata conforms to a standard format with the relief portrait in a niche set in an architectural frame; the inscriptional plaque is below. It dates to the mid or late second century C.E. and served to commemorate her death at the grave or tomb. The epitaph reads: "Dedication to the gods and departed spirits. Lutatia Lupata aged sixteen. Lutatia Severa (set this up) in memory of her foster-daughter. Here she lies. May the Earth rest lightly upon you" (*AE* 1959.0029). Note that letters are irregularly formed and lines slant – indications of a restricted budget and lower status.

elite classes, so the mixing of motives here – of maternal sentiment and economic dependence, or even exploitation – was not out of place. At first glance the representation of the girl with the lute brings to mind the sophistication of Pliny's wife, but the juxtaposition of image and inscription may indicate a very different social context in which families were broken up, children were lost and found, and women worked in sordid and risky trades that operated beneath the radar of the moralists and politicians in the city of Rome.

Dying Before Their Time

Laments over the sad fates of girls who died just as they were about to be wed are commonplace in the sources (epitaphs, poems, and letters). That the most numerous evidence of girls' lives concerns their premature deaths does not indicate that the majority of girls expired as brides-to-be but, rather, that these deaths were most consistently and poignantly documented. Both the archaeological and literary sources reflect social biases and attitudes: as marriage provided the culminating rite of passage for adulthood, girls who died unmarried were deprived of a significant element of their social identity. As it is common for epitaphs to record the age of deceased children as, for example, "twelve years, eleven months, twenty-eight days"; that is, at just before reaching the milestone of the next year, so, too, do accounts of young women conform to the *topos* or pattern of the death of a maiden in which mourning at the funeral has replaced the joy brought on by the wedding plans. Their short lives became all the more bittersweet when seen in terms of the future that they were denied. Funerary monuments not only honor the deceased's short life but occasionally represent a prospective view as consolation: the altar of Julia Victorina has two portraits carved in relief, one on the front and the other on the back, that depict the deceased as a girl at the time of her death and then as the woman that she would never become (Figures 28 and 29).

Death was a fact of life for Roman children and their parents. It is estimated that about one quarter of infants died before reaching their first birthday, and half of all children died by the age ten. Given the unrelenting devastation of childhood illnesses, parents were hardened by experience, it is thought, and tended not to commemorate infants or very young children much (grieving parents refusal to invest in monuments and epitaphs, however, may not suggest a lack of feeling for the very brief lives lost to them). Their attachment to older children and adolescents, however, is reflected in the funerary monuments dedicated to them, although their number and accompanying epitaphs tend to represent an urban, affluent population, both of elites and freedpeople.

Parents, however, did commemorate the very young, and poets sang the virtues of other sweet, lost children. In the late first century C.E., the poet Martial devoted three epigrams to his favorite slave-girl, Erotion, who died at the age of five (5.34, 5.37, 10.61). In one poem, sounding like a father, he worries about her being frightened in the

28 and 29. Paris, Louvre, inv. 1443. Réunion des Musées Nationaux/Art Resource, N.Y., 17923, 17924. The funerary altar of Julia Victorina, dated to 60–70 C.E., was placed in the tomb – some altars had containers for the deceased's ashes within. The inscription reads: "To the Shades of the Departed. For Julia Victorina, who lived ten years, five months. Her parents, C. Julius Saturninus and Lucilia Procula erected this for the sweetest daughter" (*CIL* 6.20727). Note the full face and boyish hairstyle in the bust on the top, and the rather elongated face with a pronounced bone structure and more elaborate coiffure on the bottom – both portraits are shown wearing identical earrings.

underworld and wishes that his darling may play and prattle his name (5.34). In another, he expresses his love for the girl whose beauty outshone eastern pearls and whose breath was as sweet as honey, terms of comparison that evoke romantic relationships (5.37). Furthermore, Martial compares his deep grief for the girl to that of a disapproving colleague who has lost his wealthy wife, whose fortune continues to support him. Martial's affection for Erotion is held up as a far finer thing. The contours of his relationship to the girl are not clear to us: masters and mistresses occasionally kept select slave children from the household staff as their "pets," that is, favorites upon whom they lavished attention and treats. The attraction was sexual or, at least, erotic in some of these relationships, although owners also looked after their little charges with parental concern (and even considered them as foster-daughters and -sons).

In a letter written in 105 or 106 C.E., the younger Pliny informs an acquaintance of the death of the daughter of a mutual friend Fundanus. The girl, Minicia Marcella, was not quite fourteen – note the language of epitaphs here, with the years ratcheted up to the round number to evoke the premature demise, unfulfilled promise, and unspoken vows. She "combined the wisdom of age and dignity of womanhood with the sweetness and modesty of youth and innocence . . . she loved her nurses, her attendants and her teachers, . . . she applied herself intelligently to her books and was moderate and restrained in her play. She bore her last illness with patient resignation and, indeed, with courage" (*Epistles* 5.16, trans. B. Radice). Pliny catalogues virtues revealing a girl on the cusp of womanhood with an affectionate and buoyant nature bolstered by a self-control and resolve that allow her to face death with forbearance. Death was all the more cruel because Minicia Marcella was engaged to be married, and her father was left with the sad task of replacing the orders for her wedding finery with those for the funeral. Pliny borrows from the theme of the death of the maiden here, and then finishes the letter with an account of Fundanus' intense grief for his daughter.

In 1881 a funerary altar dedicated to "Minicia Marcella Fundani f(ilia)," (Minicia Marcella, daughter of Fundanus), was uncovered outside

of Rome. It was an extraordinary find because rarely can we match literary and archaeological material so closely. Unfortunately for art historians, the front of the altar consists of the epitaph without a portrait carved
in relief. The epitaph, however, contradicts Pliny and states that the girl
lived to be twelve years, eleven months, and seven days. Did Pliny get
it wrong? It is more likely that, in the literary genre of the letter, Pliny
aimed for an emotional reaction by referring to Minicia Marcella's age as
not yet fourteen, the age thought to represent the division between childhood and adolescence. He portrays a girl in transition. The ages recorded
here are worth noting: an elite girl of twelve – or nearly thirteen – was
engaged to be married with the date of the wedding fast approaching.

Other funerary altars from tombs provide images of young brides
and girls in transition. The altar of Minucia Suavis has a portrait carved
in relief contained within niche in a format similar to that of Lutatia
Lupata's altar (Figure 30). The altar has a relief portrait with soft and
delicate features that complement the meaning of the girl's *cognomen*,
Suavis as sweet or pleasant. The portrait exhibits striking features: the
wide face of a girl with large eyes set far apart framed by crisply carved
lids, along with prominent cheekbones, and full, bow-shaped lips. The
mingling of both childish and more mature features, the full cheeks and
well-defined jawline, suggests the girl's stage of life as a teenager. The
epitaph tells us that Minucia Suavis was married at her tender age of
fourteen, which seems young for a girl from the lower orders (her father
may have been a slave when she was born because she does not share
his family name, Claudius; Suavis was also a slave's name, appropriate
for its invocation of a docile and obedient servant). Although her husband's name is given, it is her "most pious" father who erected the
altar. Why didn't the husband commemorate his young wife? We can
only speculate that the wedding was so recent that Minucia Suavis still
seemed closer to her own family or that her husband could not afford
to fulfill his duties toward his departed wife. Clearly this funerary altar
seems to document a girl in transition, not merely from this world to
the next, but between the house of her own father and that of her
husband.

30. Rome, Museo Nazionale Romano, chiostro, ala IV, inv. 30. Altar of Minucia
Suavis, ca. 50–75 C.E. The oval face with its delicate features bears marks of
idealization as if the artist had modified the subject's features through a template of
preferred good looks – compare with the rather plain portrait of Lutatia Lupata on
her altar (Figure 27). The inscription reads: "To the Shades of the Departed. For
Minucia Suavis, (wife of) P. Sextilius Campanus, lived fourteen years, eight months,
twenty-three days. Tiberius Claudius Suavis, her most pious father, erected this"
(*CIL* 6.22560).

Matchmaking

The selection of a husband was a family affair that began early. For first marriages in which aristocratic daughters were betrothed as early as twelve or thirteen, the parents' wishes were paramount in making a decision; it could not be otherwise given that sheltered and chaperoned girls had no opportunities for making a romantic match of their own (Figure 31). Although others contrived occasions to meet boys – the late republican poet Sulpicia portrays the intensity of a premarital love affair as she scolds her guardian for trying to take her away from Rome (and her lover) on a birthday outing:

> My hateful birthday has arrived, and I have to spend the dismal day without Cerinthus in the tiresome countryside. What is more delightful than the city? Do you really think a villa or a cold stream in the farm country of Arezzo suits a girl? Now relax your excessive concern for my welfare, Mesalla. Journeys, uncle, are often ill-timed. Carried off, I leave here my soul and my senses, though you do not allow me to live according to my wish. ([Tib.] 3.14, trans. A. Keith)

The persuasive and strong-minded Sulpicia gets her way as the trip is postponed. It is interesting that she mentions her lover to her guardian rather than keeping the romance a secret. Her poems, however, did not constitute a diary recording the events of an actual love affair. Yet, the

31. London, British Museum, second-fourth centuries C.E. HIP/Scala/ Art Resource, N.Y., 179774. Bethrothal rings representing the gesture of *dextrarum iunctio*, the clasped hands, as a symbol of marriage in the center of the group.

forthright character and worldliness of her literary persona should make us pause when we consider the cloistered lives of Roman girls and young women.

Matrons had greater say in the selection of their daughters' second or third husbands if they were widowed and had borne the three children that allowed them exemption from a guardian (if not, there was a guardian or, perhaps, two: one for the mother and another for the daughter, depending on the type of marriage the mother had entered). Yet, there are examples in which the bride's wishes were subjected to the concerns for political alliances between families or for the sake of property or social connections. The latter two motivations also involved not only the elites but those who would like to move in their circles, that is, the equestrians and freedmen in the towns and provinces. For families without much property, less was at stake, but shopkeepers' daughters probably tended to marry the sons of shopkeepers, and farmers' daughters wound up with men who tilled the soil. Perhaps some freedom of choice in the selection of partners was available only to those at the bottom of society (however, male slaves were occasionally given partners as rewards by their masters): slaves in large households often formed informal sexual relationships (*contubernia*) that could be made into legal unions if they were subsequently freed by their masters; masters encouraged and condoned these relationships as they increased their staff and improved morale, while others bred slaves like cattle (Varro 1.17.5–6 and 2.9.5–8). Soldiers, although forbidden to marry before 197 c.e., took on common-law wives who followed the troops.

Mothers also took responsibility for their daughter's matches. The most well-known example is Terentia, Cicero's wife, who allowed her daughter, Tullia, to choose her third husband, Dolabella, when Cicero was away serving as governor of a province. Tullia (79–45 b.c.e.) had already been married twice, in her teens to her first husband who widowed her, and then to an aristocrat from whom she was divorced fairly quickly. The union with Dolabella fared no better: the couple lived separately after their first unsuccessful pregnancy and during a subsequent pregnancy, Cicero lobbied for a divorce so that Tullia and her mother could raise the baby without Dolabella's intervention. Financial complications made the divorce impossible but Cicero's desire for a grandchild was not to be: Tullia died after her son was born and the child probably died soon after. Cicero's grief for his daughter was heartfelt as he expressed it in letters and in his desire to build a monument in her memory (*Att. 12*, trans. Shackleton Bailey). The life of Tullia was not uncommon: several marriages, no issue, and death from childbirth.

The poet Statius, trying to convince his wife of the benefits of moving from Rome to Naples in the 90s C.E., asserts that an ample supply of husbands for her daughter (from a previous marriage) are available in Naples. Statius sums up his stepdaughter and her chances with these words: "because alone and unmarried she is wasting her youth and beauty in barren leisure. . . . Nor is it only Rome that is fruitful in marriage unions and blazing festal torches: in my country too are sons-in-laws found" (*Silvae* 3.5. 60–71, trans. J. H. Mozley). The wife's reluctance to move from her house in metropolitan Rome to a lesser city suggests that mothers had keen interests in their daughters' futures and were inclined to act on their behalf.

Weddings

The Roman wedding was a celebration that introduced the couple to the community and a ritual that initiated the civic duties and social expectations of marriage with elements of spectacle. As men were typically in their later twenties at their first marriage, they were establishing themselves in careers or, at least, beginning to make a mark. For girls in their mid-to-upper teens (and some at more tender ages, as we have seen), their wedding was also their debut in society. Before being married, they were to put aside childish things, toys and dolls, and to weave a special tunic, a *tunica reta* along with a yellow hairnet, on an old-fashioned upright loom to be worn on the night before the wedding. The first stipulation indicates that the brides were still considered to be children, and the second demonstrates the pervasive ideology of woolwork in that weaving was a requirement for the bride, with an examination to be passed under stringent conditions of working an out-of-date loom. As the historical and literary sources on wedding rites sought to explain the meaning of archaic customs, it is not clear whether these rites were actually performed in the late republic and empire with any frequency or were charming antiques revived in some cases for special religious purposes (see the "high" or old-fashioned marriage, the *confarreatio*, of the Flaminica Dialis in Chapter 4). A Roman wedding was not primarily a religious ritual (despite its offerings and sacrifices) but, rather, an event marking the union of a couple. Some written contracts and stipulations for dowries are extant from Roman Egypt in the first and second centuries C.E. The documents usually state that the couple will live together, the monetary value of the dowry or the possessions accompanying the bride (the former being cash or land; the latter typically fine garments, jewelry, bronze mirrors, etc.), and show the names of those who signed.

Attention was given to the bride's coiffure and costume (Figure 32). The bride wore her hair arranged in six plaited locks bound by woolen fillets in a style that recalled the coiffure of the chief priestesses, the Vestal Virgins. No doubt this severely restrained coiffure evoked the chastity of the Vestals, a less extreme version of which was cherished in wives. The bride's hair was parted by an unusual instrument, a bent spearhook. Why this peculiar and threatening substitute for a comb? Even the sources wonder about this, but surely the intrusion of a weapon at the toilette implies the husband's sexual domination of his wife and the status of Rome's first wives, the Sabine women, as the plunder of a military assault. Since rich and luxurious hair signaled a vigorous female sexuality, the bride's hair had to be tightly bound and covered out of modesty. The costume also suggested the bride's fertility and chastity: her tunic was tied with a belt of pure ewe's wool and fastened by a particular knot (called "Herculean") that was difficult to undo.

Despite the elaborate treatment of hair, the veiling of the bride's head remained central to her trousseau – the Latin verb to marry, "nubere," also means to veil oneself. Later during the ceremony, the bride unveiled herself to her husband and his family, as if to reveal herself as the genuine

32. Rome, Vatican Museums. Scala/Art Resource, N.Y., 139937. The Aldobrandini Wedding Painting (detail) decorated the wall of a Roman house in the late or early first centuries B.C.E.–C.E. The bride's deep yellow veil is folded on the bed, while she prepares for the wedding ceremony with the goddess Venus at her side.

article under the disguise. The bride's unveiling occurred as the couple stood face to face. Then the bride may have uttered the ritual words, "*Ubi tu Gaius, ego Gaia*" ("where you are the male, I am the female"), to declare herself the wife of her husband in a marriage evoked as a union of two complementary halves (or this could have occurred later when she entered the bridegroom's house). The couple's right hands were joined in observance of their obligations and trust (a marriage contract was often signed and sealed at the wedding). After the couple made a sacrifice and shared a special cake of grain, the wedding feast probably took place.

The procession of the bride from her house to that of her husband (*deductio in domum mariti*) provided a spectacle that served as a wedding announcement. Led by three young boys who had living mothers (probably considered favorable for the bride's anticipated maternity), the bride in all her finery, and with ubiquitous spindles or distaffs in hand instead of a bouquet, passed through the streets. Torches were lit, with one of white pine preceding the bride in honor of Ceres, goddess of the fertile earth, and the Sabine women, whose abduction was illuminated by the same torches. The sight of the bride and her entourage may have aroused excitement and curiosity, even to the point of eliciting rude or obscene comments from passersby, another activity considered to be auspicious in the sources – think of the rowdy and lewd behavior expected in bachelor parties. Nuts were tossed and an archaic salutation, "Talasio," cried out, another tradition from the Sabine episode, so clearly the founding myth of Roman marriage.

Once at the husband's house, the bride is carried across the threshold by her attendants, not the bridegroom. She adorned the posts at the doorway with wool and smeared them with fat to elicit wealth and well-being for the couple. Our picture of the wedding ceremony has to be pieced together from a number of sources, so the ceremony remains a collage with some activities, no doubt, no longer practiced as others became so commonplace that they may not have been thought worthy of mention. The bridegroom presented the bride with fire and water as basic elements of life, another evocation of the purpose of marriage as a productive enterprise through the raising of children and maintenance of property.

Husbands and Wives.

We can expect a wide variation in the relationships reported between husbands and wives from the late republican through the high imperial periods, in different regions of the empire, and in various genres from funerary epitaphs to legal codes or satire. Although the official line on marriage did not admit to sentiment, as we have seen, the emotions of married couples can be gleaned from select sources. Some observations can be made about the structure of the relationship before looking at a few specific cases of the bonds between man and wife. The age differences of bride and groom are important to note. The bride was expected to establish herself as a wife to an older man who may also have had a mother (and father) living in the house or nearby. Whether the mother-in-law served as a guide to the intricacies of household management or as the bride's prison guard, the situation was rife with tension. Granted that elite Romans typically didn't allow their girls the liberty or leisure to indulge in adolescent escapades, one may question the bride's emotional readiness for the marriage bed and early motherhood, let alone the public duties of matrons in aristocratic families.

From our point of view, elite Roman marriages look like business deals or political alliances between prominent houses. There was room, however, for affection in arranged marriages, even though this was not the purpose of the match. Philosophers spoke of the ideal marriage in which husbands and wives could provide companionship for one another; if this seems strikingly obvious, recall that it would only be possible among elite couples in which the wife had some education and possessed the leisure to devote the time to share her husband's interests in letters and philosophy (for example, in the relationship of Calpurnia and the younger Pliny, and see the high-powered careers of Livia and the elder Agrippina in Chapter 4). That this concept appears in philosophical contexts suggests that amicable, affectionate relations among spouses of the lower social orders were not of interest to the authors and readers of these high-minded texts. In the letters of the younger Pliny and of the stoic philosopher Musonius Rufus, the weakness of wives as touted by moralists and satirists is not evident. Rather, virtuous matrons could also be intelligent, responsible, and trustworthy partners in marriages that allotted a balance of power, although good wives were always expected to defer to their husbands with the proper expression of feminine modesty and reserve (Figure 33).

Sentiments about married life from the spouses themselves are hard to come by, and it was only at the end of their lives as couples that we have a few phrases characterizing their virtues inscribed on the stones marking their tombs. The formulaic quality of funerary epitaphs, their staid praise of good women and lack of personal voices, frustrates our inquiry into the emotional bonds of marriage. It was expected that survivors conform to stiff social expectations in inscriptions erected in public as the final words to a loved one, but personal letters reveal the flicker of passing moods amid the humming activity of daily life and its crises. That husbands and wives loved each other and longed for their missing spouse, away on business or family visits, is expressed with the appropriate passion in letters. The younger Pliny's letters, as we have seen, offer insight into the social life and mentality of the upper class in the early second century C.E. Better known for articulating the concerns and values of the leading men of his day, his letters only very occasionally stray into the domain of feelings. Here is Pliny writing to his absent wife:

> You cannot believe how much I miss you. I love you so much, and we are not used to separations. So I stay awake most of the night thinking of you, and by day my feet carrying me (a true word, carrying) to your room at the times I usually visited you; then finding it empty I depart, as sick and sorrowful as a lover locked out. The only time I am free from this misery is when I am in court and wearing myself out with my friends' lawsuits. You can judge then what a life I am leading, when I find my rest in work and distraction in troubles and anxiety. (*Epistles* 7.5, trans. B. Radice)

This letter provides a rare account of physical longing for a wife, especially noteworthy in the words of the younger Pliny. The sleepless nights, the involuntary visits to her rooms, and the reference to the lover locked out derive from the love poetry of the first century B.C.E. and give the letter a literary quality, which does not render the emotional appeal less sincere. For a man of Pliny's education and background, the language of love poetry provided a format for expressing his desire, for identifying the symptoms, and heightening their effects of his suffering. Clearly Pliny does not stoop as low as the miserable lovers of the poems because he goes on to say that he continued with his rounds in court, his work being his only relief from his sadness. The juxtaposition of the affairs of the heart and the world of work and duty, *negotium*, is characteristic of a man of Pliny's caliber, who was always in demand.

33. New York, Metropolitan Museum of Art, inv. 38.27. Altar of Cominia Tyche, ca. 85–100 C.E., dedicated by her husband Lucius Annius Festus for his "chaste and loving wife," as described in the inscription (*CIL* 6. 16054). The relief portrait of Cominia Tyche, who died at the age of twenty-seven years, eleven months, and twenty-eight days, features a severe expression, perhaps indicative of her superior character, more closely modeled on the male virtues of integrity, dignity, and self-restraint.

Letters written on papyrus in Roman Egypt have survived in extraordinary numbers because of the dry desert climate, and the corpus of texts on papyrus scrolls includes letters written (or dictated to scribes) by women. The women, many of whom were staying on farms in the countryside of the Fayum while their husbands were working in Alexandria in the first and second centuries C.E., sent off messages to husbands, mothers, and children (see map). Many of these refer to the banal necessities of life, the making of clothing, the preparation of foodstuffs, estate management, and travel (which women seem to have done frequently on their own, to visit family, go to weddings, see new babies, bring home the dead, etc.). A number of women's letters were found in the archive of Apollonios, the *strategos* or chief civil administrator in a district of Upper Egypt during the Jewish revolt of 115–117 C.E. Apollonios's wife

Aline wrote to her husband while he was on military service during the revolt:

> Aline to my dear Apollonios, many greetings. I am very wor-
> ried for you on account of the things that people reported about
> what is happening and because you left so suddenly. I take no
> pleasure in food and drink, but always stay awake day and night
> with only one thought, your safety. Only my father's care revives
> me and, by your safety, I lay without eating on New Year's Day,
> until my father came and forced me to eat. I beg you, therefore,
> to look after your safety, and not to face danger alone with-
> out a guard. But do the same as the strategos here who puts
> the burden on the magistrates. . . . " (trans. R. Cribiore, *C. Pap.
> Jud.* 436)

Aline experiences the terrors no doubt experienced by many other wives of soldiers and officers. That she is revived by her father indicates that he must have been nearby and concerned about his adult daughter, whose well-being he does not neglect just because she is a married woman. It is telling that she asks her husband to take advantage of his position of authority and leave the dangerous duty to his subordinates, a privilege that Apollonios would not claim as a man of honor and integrity, so it seems. We hear the voice of a very anxious woman who appeals to her husband for his safety and her peace of mind.

Funerary art, in conjunction with the epitaphs, offers the most complete record of conjugal devotion, despite the drawbacks of the genre. The proper commemoration of a spouse with tomb, epitaph, and statuary was a public act that reflected the family's financial status, as well as their sense of propriety and obligation to the deceased's memory, which was the purpose of the monument. The attention to displays of fine architecture and to protocol did not necessarily indicate that emotions were secondary in the commemorative process, although they mostly remain hidden from us beneath the marble surfaces and ritual acts. An example of a sculpture representing the deceased reclining on a couch or

34. London, British Museum, inv. 2335. Kline sculpture of a married couple from the early second century C.E. The woman's head was broken off and reattached, so the angle of its tilt may not be original. Some kline sculptures had hollow cavities in the back in which to place an ash urn for the deceased's remains. The poet Martial describes a wife transporting her dead husband's bones back from Cappadocia, Turkey: ". . . and when to the tomb she envies she was giving that sacred urn, she deemed herself twice widowed of her ravished spouse" (*Epigrams* 9.30, trans. W. Ker).

kline suggests the importance of commemorating a spouse with a funerary monument (Figure 34). Although the *kline* sculpture typically depicts the deceased reclining at a banquet or asleep as in final repose, here the reclining figure is depicted holding a bust of her spouse. A sequence of events is conflated in this format: the full-length reclining figure represents the most recently deceased wife while the bust that she embraces depicts the husband who died before her; the bust provides proof that she perpetuated his memory with a fine monument and wishes to be remembered in the act of wifely devotion cradling the work of art, the effigy of her husband. There can be no better indication of how works of art were invested with emotion than this representation of the wife reclining not with her husband but with the marble bust depicting him. The monument is striking as a work of art about the powers of evocation of art, how the sculptural form of the bust stands for the departed husband and is tenderly embraced or proudly displayed.

Among the lower social orders, conjugal devotion was also represented in funerary reliefs once decorating the facades of tombs. A funerary relief from Rome depicts a butcher and his wife united by a warm gesture (Figure 35). The center of the relief panel shows the togate husband facing his veiled wife, who raises his hand to her lips (a pun on her name, Philematium, which means little kiss). The gesture expresses the wife's devotion to the husband she loves. The striking emotional content suggests her respect, admiration, and, above all, her subservience to her husband. The lengthy text, in two columns on either side of the image, allows them to speak (the husband's is in the left column):

> I am Lucius Aurelius Hermia, freedman of Lucius, and a butcher from the Viminal Hill. This woman, chaste in body, who preceded me in death, my one and only wife, (who) lovingly presided over my soul, she lived, faithful to a faithful husband (who had) equal devotion, since no selfishness ever kept her from her duty.

The wife also speaks (in the right column):

> While I was living I was called Aurelia Philematium. I was chaste, modest, with no knowledge of the ways of the world, and faithful to my husband. My husband was my fellow-freedman of the same master, of whom – alas! – I am now deprived. In fact and in truth, he was more like a father to me. When I was seven years old he took me on his lap, but at forty I was taken by death. He flourished in the eyes of all thanks to my steadfast devotion. *CIL* 6. 9499 (trans. M. Roller)

Their names, Lucius Aurelius Hermia and Aurelia Philematium, indicate that they both were once slaves of Lucius Aurelius, who had freed them. Aurelius had looked after Philematium since she was a little

35. London, British Museum, inv. 2274. Funerary Relief of Lucius Aurelius Hermia and his wife, Aurelia Philematium, first century B.C.E. Their Greek origins, characteristic of slaves, are revealed in their names: while Hermia derives from the god Hermes, which signified good luck in business, Philematium means a little kiss and is, therefore, appropriate to this touching scene.

girl, but we don't know when his fatherly attentions turned amorous or if their union preceded their manumission (Aurelius's care for her also raises the question of motherhood in the slave household: had the girl's mother died or was she sold off from the household?). Aurelia Philematium died at age forty and was survived by Aurelius, who must have been considerably older. Chastity, modesty, fidelity, and devotion are the virtues that defined the exemplary matron, the ranks of which Philematium joined in death as in life. Despite her low status as a freed-woman and butcher's wife, she appeared to aspire to the traditional ideals of womanhood. Unlike the representation of the matron's devotion in the *kline* monument, Aurelius is not depicted in the scene in the act of commemorating his wife, rather, it is his previously deceased wife who demonstrates her reverence to him and her dependence on him from an early age. Of course, since Aurelius commissioned the relief, we only see Philematium through his portrayal of her as "faithful to a faithful husband."

Motherhood

No children are mentioned in the epitaphs of the butcher and his wife, although this by itself is not unusual in the corpus of funerary reliefs in which husbands and wives commemorated each other. In fact, it is offset by the numerous inscriptions dedicated by parents commemorating children who died at an early age. The statistics of death (although distorted by the overrepresentation of predominantly urban and affluent artisans and professionals) offer a rough sketch of Roman patterns of fertility: high rates of infant and childhood mortality drove high birth rates. It has been estimated that a Roman woman had to bear at least five babies in order to ensure that two of them would survive to adulthood (Figure 36). If the scourge of childhood diseases did not take their toll, then military service for young men and childbirth for young women endangered them. Thus, the young matron would have spent most of her early married life pregnant, a condition considered to have been optimal by the medical authorities. The gynecologist Soranus, practicing in Rome in the early second century C.E., expressed misgivings about the conventional wisdom encouraging frequent pregnancy and realized that this also brought women closer to disease and death from infection, hemorrhage, and fever (*Gynecology*, 1.30–32, trans. O. Temkin).

Since the begetting and raising of children was the purpose of marriage, pregnancy was usually a desired state, especially in a society in which young life was so fragile. As always, some pregnancies were unwanted, inconvenient, or disastrous to the woman's health or honor. Contraception was practiced in the form of potions, douches or vaginal pessaries, some of which contained spermicidal ingredients, such as vinegar and brine; other methods fall into the popular self-help category of home remedies. Women who wished to abort were advised to leap and shake, and to take various herbs (Soranus, *Gynecology*, 1.64–65). Abortion was not illegal (until the third century C.E.), although abortifacients were banned under the law of poisons (along with aphrodisiacs), and quasi-medical procedures were seen to be the remedy of fashionable and immoral women of the capital.

36. York, Yorkshire Museum. Tombstone of Flavia Augustina, third century C.E., with an inscription informing us that both children died young, one before two years, the other at one year and three days; Flavia Augustina died at the age of thirty-nine and the family was commemorated by her husband and the children's father, a military veteran (*CIL* 7.245).

The early stages of pregnancy may have gone unnoticed by inexperienced women without the benefits of medical technology or even a schedule of regular periods due to malnutrition or hard labor. Elite women were not spared from ignorance: the younger Pliny writes of his young wife who, unaware that she was pregnant, did not take the proper steps to avoid a miscarriage (*Epistles* 8.10–11). Other wives took advantage of their state – Augustus's daughter Julia, notorious for her alleged promiscuity, claimed that her pregnancies allowed her to engage in extramarital affairs without fear of conception, "I never take on a passenger unless the ship is full" (Macrobius 2.5.9, trans. A. Richlin). For most women, however, pregnancy was a state of anticipation without the

37. Naples, Museo Archeologico Nazionale, 113264.
Alinari/Art Resource N.Y., 72752. Vaginal speculum for
dilation of the cervix that made gynecological examinations
possible, first century C.E.

comfort of an estimated due date since ancient physicians believed that
a full term lasted nine or ten months. They also believed that a seventh-
month child could survive, but the eighth-month child seemed to fare
less well (Figure 37). Soranus advises women from their fourth to seventh
months to eat well and partake of light exercise, such as vocal exercises,
reading aloud, and promenades (all leisure activities of the affluent), in
order to be strong enough to withstand labor. He scorns most super-
stitions held dear by midwives who supervised the deliveries yet warns
that visual stimuli could affect the development of the fetus: an expectant mother who contemplates statuary will have well-formed children,
whereas one who spies a monkey will bear hairy and lanky-armed babies!
(*Gynecology* 1.55, 1.49, 1.54, 1.39).

Few women saw physicians during their pregnancies because midwives routinely provided affordable medical care with the familiar faces
of women from the neighborhood or district. Midwives were slaves kept
in the grand households or freedwomen, a few of whom earned enough
to erect tombs in which they commemorated themselves and their profession (Figure 38). The midwife traveled to her patient's home when
she was in labor and brought her own equipment, including the birthing
chair in which the expectant mother sat in order to push the infant out
and down through the hole cut in the seat. The midwife's care for her
patient was revealed in her touch, so Soranus recommends that they have

soft skin, long fingers, and short nails (*Gynecology*, 1.4). It was literally a "hands-on" profession in which physical contact and trust weighed heavily. Yet when a mother died or an infant born disfigured, the midwife's intimacy with the family and her supervision of a mysterious and misunderstood act often resulted in her being blamed – charges of witchcraft were levied against midwives when families lost confidence. We may assume that many more women delivered at home – or in the backrooms of shops, alleys, or fields – unattended.

38. Ostia, Museo Ostiense, inv. 5204. Scala/Art Resource, N.Y., 47894. Terracotta relief from the Tomb of Scribonia Attice, mid–second century c.e. The inscription on the tomb indicates that the tomb was intended for the midwife, her surgeon husband, and her mother. The relief depicts a standing assistant, who steadies the woman in labor, while the midwife sits on a lower stool, either turning away to preserve the patient's modesty or to appeal to the viewer.

Tradition stipulated that the newborn child was placed on the floor and left to cry for a while, before being cleaned and swaddled. Another ritual prompted the father to pick up the infant to signal his acceptance of the child as his own (he was not required to do so – unwanted children or those deemed insufficiently healthy to raise were routinely abandoned in the garbage dumps on the outskirts of cities). Naming of the infant, however, was delayed, no doubt, because of the infant's tenuous hold on life in the first week. A baby girl would be named on the eighth day, a boy on the ninth, accompanied by rites of purification. In the republic, girls took the family name and were distinguished from their sisters by the epithet "elder" or "younger" or ordinal numbers "prima," "secunda," etc., to mark their place in the family. In the empire, they had two names, the first being the family name, the second derived from their father's name.

Mothers and Daughters

Mothers took part in their daughters' lives after they married and moved away. They were repositories of wisdom on household economy and on the education or training of children, on the management of farms or shops, and on religious ritual, among other topics. They visited each other in their houses and went out together, as a document from the corpus of Egyptian papyri demonstrates. The farmer Hippalos, son of Archis, petitions his local police chief that his wife and her mother were assaulted and robbed of jewelry and valuables in the village bathhouse (*P.Ryl. II 124*, first century C.E.). If the women were escorted by their slaves, they were of no help in fending off the attack during the soak and sauna (the ancient equivalent of a spa session).

Other women traveled further afield on business: in a letter a woman named Eutychis writes to her mother Ametrion about her delay in arriving – she is traveling with freight and has been refused by camel drivers and now is waiting for a boat to take her to her mother (*P.Oxy.* XIV.1773, third century C.E.). She also directs her mother to make certain cash transfers for her, but, unfortunately, the letter does not indicate what

39. Paris, Louvre, inv. 1331; photo courtesy of H.R. Goette. Altar of Julia Secunda and Cornelia Tyche, ca. 150–165. The altar was originally larger but carved down to size in the modern period. The epitaph on the right side that tells us about their deaths is preserved in texts, but is now no longer extant (*CIL* 6. 20674). The altar's pediment represents two empty chairs and the attributes of goddesses, the bow and quiver of Diana for Julia Secunda, and the cornucopia, torch, rudder, wheel of Fortuna – Tyche means "fortune" in Greek, so this is a reference to the goddess who ultimately failed the unfortunate Cornelia Tyche.

type of goods she is carrying nor for what purpose they require transport (Wool to be woven? Merchandise for a family business?). Eutychis appears to have been traveling without her husband or any male escort of her status.

Funerary art also testifies to the bonds between mothers and daughters in life and death, and a few monuments honor them (although the daughters were younger and unmarried in order for them to be commemorated by their fathers; for exceptions, see Figure 30 and the "Matchmaking" section on Cicero's Tullia). A funerary altar commemorates a mother and daughter who were lost at sea during a storm (Figure 39). The two women are represented on the altar as portrait busts, including the shoulders and upper arms and resting on bases decorated with acanthus leaves. Their hair is elaborately arranged in the fashions of the mid–second century C.E. in styles appropriate to a maiden with her

40 and 41. Cairo, Egyptian Museum, CG 33237 and CG 33240, photos courtesy of
Steve Vinson. The mummy portraits of Demo and little girl, late first century C.E.,
were found together so are assumed to be mother and daughter. The painted
portraits reflect hairstyles and other modes of adornment popular in metropolitan
Rome and, thus, add a dimension to the study of Roman portraiture.

hair simply parted and swept back and to a matron with braids wound
high on top (both of these styles were worn by imperial women, the
elder and younger Faustinas). As in the *kline* sculpture, funerary altars
and relief often depict the deceased in the form of expensive and prestigious works of art. The images of the busts on the altar may have
alluded to the presence of busts in the women's tomb or, in fact, may
have provided a substitute for art works that were out of the family's
financial reach. Either way, the representation of portrait busts suggests
that the husband and father, Julius Secundus, intended to commemorate
the women properly.

The epitaph gives us their names and ages: Julia Secunda (on the left) was not yet twelve years old and Cornelia Tyche (on the right) not yet forty when they died. Their ship went down in the Gulf of Leon, far from their home in the city of Rome (the altar's findspot). They may have ventured out to visit relatives in Spain, never to return. The bereft husband, Julius Secundus, was left with the sad task of mourning both wife and daughter. He chose to honor their memory with the same monument.

The mummified remains of the dead in Roman Egypt were adorned with painted portraits covering their faces (Figures 40 and 41). Painted in encaustic (pigment suspended in wax) on wooden boards (or less frequently, on the linen wrapping of the mummy itself), the mummy portraits are so richly colored and subtly shaded that they appear lifelike. The images of mother and daughter resemble one another with their round faces, big dark eyes, thick noses, and full lips. The mother's jewelry, the pearls earrings, the emerald beads, and gold chain, shimmer with light (recall the fight in the baths for jewels above). The little girl also wears a necklace of crescent-shaped drops, which symbolized fertility – appropriate for her while she was alive but heartbreaking in this state. A canvas band across the mother's mummy was inscribed, "Demo, age twenty-four, remembered forever." And so she is.

CHAPTER 3

WOMEN'S WORK

Most of the labor performed by women across the social spectrum was not recognized as work or, if done for wages or profit, was considered lowly or sordid by elite males. Domestic work, mostly performed by slaves, and commercial activities, for example, sales jobs in shops or the manufacturing of luxury or humble goods, did not merit attention because of the social status of its practitioners. Learned professions were considered anomalous for women, so female teachers and poets were usually ignored (and the fields of entertainment – or even business – considered glamorous now were off-limits to respectable women). Of course, the most noble of occupations, politics and the military, excluded women, even those of aristocratic heritage. The mistresses of the great households in Rome or the wives of military commanders on the frontiers appeared to do little besides supervising their staff of slaves; yet, their air of leisure masked the social duties and public responsibilities that fell heavily on them. Although the ancient sources did not consider these activities as entailing effort or expertise, we should acknowledge the impressive administrative and managerial skills of these women. Archaeological evidence offers glimpses of the industry that maintained households as well as cities but remains invisible in most literary sources.

The Domestic Arts

The household was the locus for the production and maintenance of many goods and services: the spinning of fibers and weaving of cloth into garments (equated with moral purity) and the curing of olives or the making of cheese and wine for home consumption are only a few of the goods routinely produced in kitchens that we would typically purchase in shops. The larger the household, the more specialized the staff for highly rarefied needs: the imperial household under Livia, the wife of Augustus, included gardeners, dressers (especially for ceremonial garments), masseuses, a silversmith, a jeweler to set pearls, a polisher of fine furniture, and a curator of paintings. The huge staff was highly stratified and organized from the bottom, the kitchen maids to those in professions, such as doctors and teachers, and all the way to the top, the stewards who supervised the daily operations of the household and its expenses. However, slaves who performed several different tasks demonstrated the shabbiness of their households. All households, even those without luxury services, served as the repositories of the family's wealth. According to traditions from Rome's agrarian origins, matrons served as keepers of the keys to the storerooms; that is, matrons were responsible for the accounts of the supplies brought in that enabled the making and processing of foodstuffs and goods. The task of household management also complemented the matron's role as a productive resource for the family as a bearer of children. Even if a steward or housekeeper supervised the shopping, the matron had to check the records and was ultimately responsible for any loss due to spoiling or theft. In a comical account of dinner at a rich freedman's house, the hostess, Fortunata, doesn't appear until after she has put the silver away and distributed leftovers to the slaves (Petronius, *Satyricon* 67). For women like Fortunata and others, wax tablets provided the means to keep accounts and manage the supplies in the larder (Figure 42).

Roman notions of domesticity and privacy differed markedly from ours, as recent research has pointed out. The Roman house (*domus*) sheltered different activities from work to play in rooms that could change their purpose according to the time of day or the needs of the occasion. Although we have been accustomed to think of home as a refuge from the world, elite Romans designed their townhouses with varying degrees of access to outsiders: bedrooms were also the scene of confidential political meetings with doorways guarded by slaves, and the *paterfamilias* was visited by clients or associates who thronged the atrium in the morning ritual of the *salutatio*, the open office hours kept by men with political clout and wealth. The house's prominence was based on its visibility and openness to the extent that doors were opened and passersby saw the crowded house during the *salutatio* as a reflection of the owner's power.

Considerations of gender are not readily apparent in the plans and archaeological remains of houses (Figure 43). The archaeological

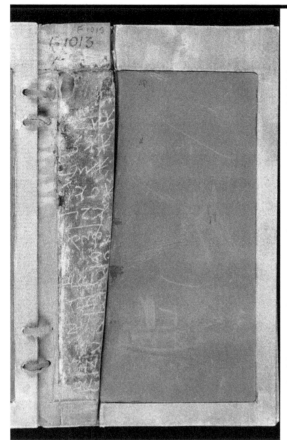

42. New Haven, Beinecke Rare Book and Manuscript Library, Yale University, P. CtYBR inv. DPm I, after D. Kleiner and S. Matheson, *I, Claudia*, figure 99. Fragment of a Waxed *Tabula* with reconstruction, second or third centuries C.E., from Dura Europos, Syria. Sheets of wax are bound in wood frames that are hinged to form a notebook. The wax would take impressions from a pointed instrument, a stylus, and then wiped flat to start over again. One needn't have been fully literate to add up sums or make simple lists on the tablets.

evidence does not indicate that there were separate women's quarters nor nurseries, although the upper floors of Roman houses (in Pompeii, for example) are not extant and may have provided greater privacy, if not seclusion for women and children. The flexible floor plans, however, allow for the moving of furniture and hanging of tapestries to keep out drafts or light so that babies and toddlers could be accommodated, perhaps, in rooms on the ground floor during the day (Figure 44). The matron may have operated out of another room also located off the atrium, in which she went over accounts, organized her staff, and did her correspondence, either by hand or with the aid of a scribe (see Chapter 2 for women's letters from Roman Egypt). Opening the house to clients and freedmen during the morning's *salutatio* required the coordination of staff to guide visitors at the door and to keep the hangers-on out of the back rooms.

Looms were set up in the atrium nearby so that the weaving was done in full daylight by slaves in sight of the matron. The spinners, who drew out the threads, could have worked anywhere in the house

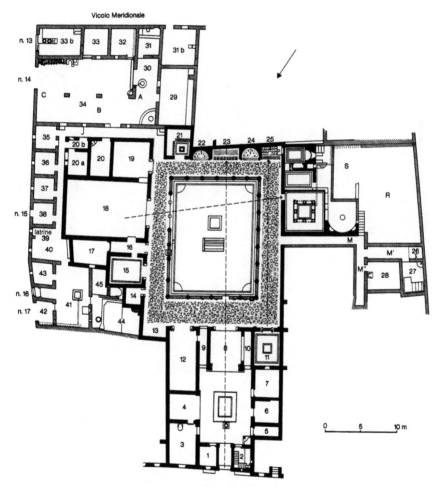

43. Pompeii, Soprintendenza. Plan of the House of the Menander in Pompeii named because of the painting in the rear of the atrium that depicts the famed dramatist. The house was built in the third century B.C.E. and renovated through the first century C.E. and includes elaborately painted dining rooms facing the peristyle court. Note the lines of sight indicating views across the peristyle.

44. Naples, Museo Archeologico Nazionale, inv. 110569. Erich Lessing/Art Resource, N.Y., 63509. Painting from House of the banker L. Caecilius Iucundus (V, 1, 26) in Pompeii, first century C.E. The painting's location near the entrance to one of the house's grandest rooms required visitors to notice the seductive scene, along with its rich colors and original applied gold for details. Erotic painting on the walls of highly trafficked rooms also suggests the principles of pleasure and power that seemed neither to shock nor embarrass nor were unfit for children's eyes. Evidently such paintings did not evince shame of the naked human body and sexual acts. Propertius remarks on the fashion for racy paintings that, he bemoans, corrupt youth; yet, his complaints are those of a jealous lover surveying the entire male population as prospective competition for his love (2.6.30–34).

and done their job while minding children, or in-between other tasks (Figure 45). Despite the reputation of woolwork as a female occupation, some weavers working in the top-tier urban households were male (as were professionals outside of the home) and the same applies for wool weighers, whose task of apportioning out the rough wool to be worked made them supervisors of the process. For the rest of society, wool-workers were female, even as wool weighers whose role complemented that of the matron in looking after the family's property. If families did not possess looms, the wool was sent to professional workshops to be woven into fabric and then cut and sewn into clothes at home (although professionals – male weavers – in shops could have done that as well).

45. London, Museum of London. The reconstruction of a Roman kitchen looks tidy and clean, but in reality the atmosphere must have been smoky from both the fire and oil lamps and hot and greasy from the stove. Hanging joints of meat, along with vegetables in baskets, would have crowded the kitchen. Fuel for the stove was stored in the niche below the platform.

46. London, British Museum. Art Resource, N.Y., 102039. The Mildenhall Treasure, a hoard of silver plate for the banquet buried for safekeeping in late Antiquity, fourth century C.E. It consists of a lavish table setting, including serving plates, bowls, dishes, candelabra, and spoons – many of these engraved with appropriate figures of revelry from classical mythology.

Workplaces are not easy to identify in houses. Looms were set up in the atrium, and spinners also could have been set to other tasks in the kitchen or with children. If weaving did not merit a dedicated space in the house, then the kitchen certainly would. Kitchens were the engines of houses and are recognized in excavations by hearths and, occasionally, masonry ovens. In villas the kitchen is often located next to the baths for the convenient supply of hot water, and in Pompeian houses, they were variously placed next to the atrium and on the periphery near the service quarters (in stately houses). The ovens and fires for gridirons posed danger in quarters crowded with wooden furnishings, textiles, and straw (ovens could also have been placed outdoors in courtyards). A reconstruction of a kitchen in the Museum of London illustrates a possible arrangement with a gridiron for a charcoal fire placed on a platform and storage space for small ceramic vessels on high shelves along with the large storage vessels, *amphorae*, on the floor; the oven is not in sight, perhaps because those in cities or towns could buy their bread in bakeries (some apartment houses shared communal ovens) (Figure 45). There are wooden tables for working, and other kitchens were stocked with tripods to hold basins.

We must imagine the kitchen of the imperial household of Livia on the Palatine hill in Rome to have been much larger but probably with less elbow room because of more elaborate equipment and numerous staff. Male cooks seem to have been the norm in grand establishments and husbands, as heads of the household, may have made the decisions in selecting menus and choosing dinner guests for the more formal affairs (Figure 46). We do know of one elite matron, Pomponia, the sister-in-law of Cicero, who was sorely put out when denied the responsibility of supervising the preparations for a meal at an estate in which the party with which she was traveling was stopping over. Cicero did not understand her indignation at being treated like a guest in her own household (*Att.* 5.3–4). Her refusal to join her

47. The Museum of Antiquities of the University and Society of Antiquities of Newcastle on Tyne, from Richmond. Everyday ware consisting of a sturdy colander, jug, and tin cup used for serving wine.

48. Ostia, Soprintendenza. Reconstructed tavern and takeout shop in Ostia on the Via di Diana, third century C.E. In the port of Rome (see map), workers could have brought home prepared food or eaten it on the premises, with its wide counters and stone benches. Women who worked in such establishments were presumed to be little better than prostitutes; yet, no doubt female customers frequented these shops as well.

husband and brother-in-law at the table indicated her resentment at not being able to manage the proceedings, organize the event, and order the food.

In less-exalted households, matrons may have selected provisions and managed mealtime preparations, while women of the lower social orders took on more of the work themselves, only resorting to their few slaves to go to the market and haul containers of oil or sacks of grain (Figure 47). Those who lived in rooms in *insulae* (blocks of buildings resembling apartment houses) without kitchen facilities may have dispensed with much of the preparations and subsisted mainly on bread and porridge, along with beans and the occasional roasted chicken from cookshops. Some greens and fruits supplemented this diet when available (Figure 48). The country wife, long celebrated for her traditional virtues, ground her own grain, baked her own coarse bread, and butchered calves for veal with the help of slaves for feast days. The ideal of rustic simplicity may not have been lost in the period of the high empire although the poets who celebrated the pastoral life never took on the backbreaking work required to maintain it.

To modern visitors of Pompeii, Herculaneum and other sites on the bay of Naples, the houses resound with emptiness. Their furnishings were lost in the intense heat and fires of the eruption of Vesuvius in 79 C.E. or ruined by being buried for centuries and then too hastily uncovered in excavations in the late eighteenth and nineteenth centuries (see map). The sculptural reliefs of the interior of a second-century sarcophagus suggest the domestic décor with a couch, tables, cupboards and shelves, with an emphasis on space for storage (Figure 49). The furniture depicted in the relief displays a costly array crowded along the walls, a substantial expenditure for those in the townhouses and beyond the means of many of those in the *insulae* apartments. Portable

49. Leiden, National Museum of Antiquities. Interior of sarcophagus from Simpelveld, Holland, early second century C.E. The abode supplies the deceased with all the comforts of home.

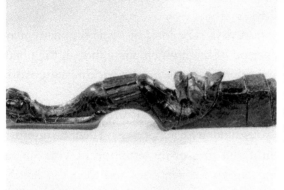

50. Dorset County Museum. Table leg from Colliton Park (shown sideways), made of shale, although most furniture was made of wood.

.394

furnishings followed the master and mistress around the house as they settled in various rooms for specific activities. One table has elaborately carved legs with a lion's or griffin's head on top and a clawed paw or hoof at the bottom, a motif that has become synonymous with classical styles in furniture design over the centuries. A similar table leg found in England shows the elegant design in a linear fashion with the compact curve of the leg balanced by the arching contours of the griffin and the claw (Figure 50). The table leg is cracked and split in places from not being well-maintained, perhaps a sign of a poorly run household (and neglect over the following centuries). Tables, such as this one extant only in its leg, were prized possessions or even family heirlooms that merited care in a world in which consumer goods were made slowly and in far fewer numbers than in a modern factory production.

Furniture also was decorated with motifs that would seem out-of-place according to our notions of domestic décor. One striking example is found in the city of Ephesus, a city with an illustrious Greek heritage on the western coast of Turkey (see map), in a block of houses sited on a ridge overlooking downtown (Figure 51). As luxurious Pompeian houses were located close to the city center, so, too, were the Terrace Houses of Ephesus, which command views of the administrative and commercial buildings and, in turn, were visible from the crowds thronging them. Arranged around peristyle courtyards like the Pompeian houses, the Terrace Houses boast of glittering mosaics on

51. Terrace House, Ephesus, second century C.E. Vanni/Art Resource, N.Y., 40119. View through the peristyle of House A.

the floors, painted murals on the walls, and some provocative furnishings. A relief panel from a frieze, in particular, stands out because of its military subject matter, better suited to a triumphal arch than to the interior it once decorated (Figure 52). The relief's representation of Trajan and his army about to face enemy forces reflects the traditions of triumphal imagery in state art that project the invincibility of imperial

52. Seljuk, Archaeological Museum, inv. 6–8/4/75, photo courtesy of H.R. Goette. The ivory relief, now darkened from age and only 8 inches (20 cm) tall, adorned the interior of the Terrace House 2 (which is a block of houses, rather than an individual dwelling). Its depiction of Trajan at war allows for a date around 116–117 C.E. or after.

soldiers bearing down on lackluster barbarians. Yet it is striking that this scene of confrontation and (impending) conquest decorated an interior of a house in Ephesus. With its Greek foundations, Ephesus was a rich port that paid homage to its Roman rulers as it had previous potentates. The battle scene may have suggested the protection Rome offered to those under its sway, a promise all the more enticing given the eastern location and Trajan's Parthian wars in the middle east. Yet, rather than appearing in a larger-than-life-size frieze on a public monument, the scene is rendered in miniature for a domestic setting, perhaps as a souvenir of major state monuments. The presence of Roman propaganda on décor may not have elicited comment from those accustomed to the ubiquitous displays of imperial might. It suggests a degree of compliance or identification with the empire on the part of its owners, members of the civic elite dependent on Roman favor. As a prestigious and precious object, the costly carving on ivory may not have aroused the same feelings of pride from the slave maids of various ethnic origins whose job was to clean and buff it; rather, they may have felt closer to the eastern soldiers amassed against the emperor. For the mistress of the house, the decorative frieze enhanced the value of her décor since motifs of public art and architecture lent prestige; yet, irreverent wives may have smirked at the image of Trajan's army, bolstering the authority of the men of the household, if not guarding the drawing room. The ivory frieze demonstrates that the home certainly was not a female domain impervious to the wider world of military action and power politics.

Childrearing

The most significant and difficult work of raising children fell to women, of course, since motherhood remained enshrined as a goal for all women. Childrearing merits discussion as women's work because enslaved, freed, and free-born women were employed as baby nurses, nannies, or governesses. Who looked after the children depended on the family's social status. Most women from the lower social orders nursed their babies and looked after their own children – some took care of others' children as well. Childhood was brief in this milieu: boys and girls were put to work at an early age at home or in the father's workshop. Some slave or freedborn girls became apprentices in trades at age twelve or thirteen. On the land, the children of tenant farmers would help out once they were big and strong enough – one assumes slave children were given tasks on estates that suited their size.

However, affluent matrons hired wet nurses to feed their babies. Wet nurses, who were slaves in the large households and hired freedwomen or freeborn women in most others, often lived with the families and stayed for up to three years while they suckled the babies of their masters or employers (Figures 53 and 54). The mother could attend to other tasks instead of constantly feeding or attending a newborn or settled baby. The historian Tacitus saw this as evidence of the decline of the moral fiber of Roman women, implying that they cared more for their figures and their leisure than for their offspring (*Germania* 20). The discussion continued later in the second century with Favorinus of Arles advocating that mothers nurse their own infants (Gellius, *Attic Nights* 12.1.17). If Favorinus, a sophist who entertained huge crowds with high-flown renditions of Greek literature, entered the debate on child care, then it was a social issue with more at stake than the feeding of babies and probably reflected anxieties about wealthy and idle matrons. Some found it repugnant that elite Roman children should spend more time in the care of servile workers than with their own mothers. Those who argued for the employment of wet nurses (even the gynecologist Soranus thought that they should be used while the mother rested after delivery, II.17) found their value in their physical hardiness and stamina, their superior milk, and their ethnic origins – Greek wet nurses being most prized because the infant nursed by them becomes accustomed to the best speech, according to Soranus (II.19).

Besides wet nurses, women with means had slave childminders to look after their sons and daughters at home, accompany them to their tutor's houses or schools, and keep them out of harm's way. As the wet-nurse performed other functions besides nursing the infant, so, too, did the other nursery staff who cared for the growing child. Male attendants,

53 and 54 (both sides of a stele). Cologne, Römisch-Germanisches Museum, inv. 122,1. Funerary Stele of the wet nurse Severina, late third century C.E. The inscription states her profession, *nutrix*, and shows her with a swaddled child in a cradle and, on the other side, breastfeeding the child.

paedogogi, may have taught the child elementary lessons but remained more of a babysitter than a tutor. Mothers hired tutors who were male, with an occasional exception of a female teacher in the provinces (see Figure 77).

Representations of childrearing are found on another form of funerary monument, sarcophagi, marble coffins with scenes carved in relief on their outer panels. Many of these scenes are mythological subjects; however, there are others that commemorate deceased children with scenes representative of their lives (Figures 55). A child's sarcophagus from the mid–second century C.E. may depict the ideal family with a sequence of scenes representing both milestones and everyday occurrences (from the left): the mother nursing her infant son from her breast under the father's intense gaze, the father tenderly holding his baby son, the son – now older – playing in a miniature wagon pulled by a goat, and the son reading to his father whose pose evokes a philosopher's concentration (Figure 56). The images representing the parent's involvement and participation in the boy's life may very well have been a fiction for most Romans of the upper social orders who were rather distant figures to their children and relied on a staff of slaves to perform the daily tasks of childrearing. In elite

55. Sarcophagus depicting children playing and riding carts with parents, second century C.E., Rome, Mus. Naz. Rom., inv. 65199, photo DAI 79.3955.

households mothers, in particular, instilled discipline in their children, cultivated traditional values, and hired their teachers, so it is striking that the figure of the father is repeated three times in rather soft focus with an emotional charge.

In a relief carved on another second-century sarcophagus, the bathing and reading scenes are juxtaposed on the short end of the box (Figure 57). Note that a slave hunches over to help the child (no longer an infant) with his bath while the mother merely looks on. This depiction of the bath is probably closer to reality in that the mother's inactivity reflects her hauteur and, thus, her status; her role is to manage the child's care through the ministrations of her slave staff – even though the tot may feel more comfortable with his lowly minders, they will be outgrown and his mother will be there to guide him as he matures. The reading scene, emblematic of the deceased child's precociousness and his bright future denied by a premature death, is placed immediately to the right of the bath. The boy, now represented at a later stage of life than that of the toddler in the bath scene, reads to a bearded and stooped-over man whose bare feet suggest that he is a schoolmaster (and not his father – compare to the footwear of the father in the reading scene

56. Paris, Louvre, photo MA 659. Réunion des Musées Nationaux/Art Resource, N.Y., 150265. The heavily restored sarcophagus of M. Cornelius Statius, mid–second century C.E., exemplifies a type of biographical narrative in which the deceased's life is summed up in a few key scenes. For adult men, scenes of political and military life provided the visual synopsis of a life; for children, the bath – the first bath of the newborn – and reading scenes were often interrupted by a playful romp. Here the bath scene has been replaced by a rare depiction of nursing by the mother rather than by a wet nurse.

57. Florence, Galleria degli Uffizi, inv. 82, photo, DAI, Rome, 57.611. A bathing and reading scene on a sarcophagus, late second century C.E. The scene was carved on the short end of the box.

of Figure 56). The father's absence is significant in its implications for childrearing in elite households carried out by many, varied surrogate parents, some warmly remembered by their young charges years later. Despite the panel's evocation of childhood, it fails as a realistic rendering because of the allegorical figures in the background: two personifications of Fate cast the child's horoscope on a globe, and a theatrical muse holds up a mask to offer inspiration to the young scholar in the reading scene. These figures enlarge the scope of the very brief life commemorated here and lend it a heroic gloss. As artifacts of children's lives and deaths, the biographical sarcophagi neither offer documentary accounts of daily life nor indulge in fantasy sequences; instead their contradictions, omissions, or idealizations may suggest concerns about raising children and, more important, parents' wishes to honor their departed sons and daughters in the best possible light.

The Arts of Cultivation

Cultivation, *cultus*, covers a range of activities that we may consider under the rubric of civilized self-improvement and collective striving from grooming and luxuries to farming and the liberal arts. Grooming and care of the female body concern us here. Cultivation of appearances was not primarily a feminine concern: men who plucked body hair and doused themselves with perfume risked being labeled effeminate while disheveled, unwashed rogues were considered rustic and uncouth. The male body, therefore, required some (but not too much) attention to appear handsome and cosmopolitan, qualities that did not come naturally. Women were also expected to maintain appearances, although aging women, in particular, came in for criticism by poets for their reliance on heavy makeup. Despite the satirists' image of women using cosmetics to entrap men (see Chapter 2), the appearance of a sophisticated, well-turned-out woman in public was cause for praise not only for herself but for her husband. Feminine beauty regimens and finery were used to transform matrons into elegant creatures worthy of the public renown or achievement of their spouses. Livy gives an account of the discussions about female extravagance and vanity, which roiled the republic, and finally allowed that feminine finery could serve as a woman's badge of honor, a display of feminine glory as a counterpart to the male honors of political office or military triumph (see Chapter 1). The literary and archaeological evidence points to a complex moral code governing female beauty, appropriate for an urbane and sophisticated culture in which appearances counted. To discount the feminine arts as repressive ideological tools or to celebrate them as means of empowerment does not adequately describe their effects, in fact, their appeal may lie in between the two extremes in practices that both established and erased social differences (e.g., between freedwomen and matrons) in ingenious and creative forms of self-expression.

Even Juvenal and Martial acknowledged the labor involved in a lady's toilette and the acquisition of clothing and jewelry in the late first and early second centuries C.E., although they sent up the misspent efforts of allegedly wretched-looking hags. The cultivation of women's appearances entailed care, labor, and control over the body in order for it to appear well groomed and elegant. Although some ancient and modern observers may not consider this as work, the ablutions and ministrations

58. Trier, Rheinisches Landesmuseum, inv. NM 184, from Neumagen. Foto
Marbura/Art Resource, N.Y., 105858. A relief from a third century C.E. funerary
monument depicts a matron at her toilette, wih four servants assisting: the first fixes
her hair, the second holds a perfume flask, the third has a mirror in hand, and the
fourth carries a water pitcher. Note the elaborate wicker chair and footstool that
supports the matron.

of the toilette suggested that beauty was a state that could be achieved
through the proper regimen. The baths, cosmetics, wigs, and costumes
signaled social position and net worth, along with submission to the
transformative powers of the makeover. For the women who could afford
these luxuries, the beauty treatment required work to make it appear as
if no work at all was involved, that the vision of loveliness was all natural.
Ovid in the *Arts of Love*, an Augustan poem of epic proportions with
advice on attracting a lover, considers the female body as providing not
only inspiration but also raw material for the artist. In art the female
form is a work in progress; yet, the artistry was performed by women in
real life (Figure 58).

Recipes for cosmetics are recorded in sources, the accounts of which
are colored by their literary genre. The elder Pliny and Ovid look to

science, magic, and their sense of the desires of women in their descriptions of creams containing such ingredients as pounded narcissus bulbs, poppies, honey, recycled incense, myrrh, fennel, dried roses, and barley water (Ovid, *Medicamina*, 51–68). Mostly vegetal and fragrant, the cosmetics could have been made at home in the kitchen or supplied by shops. The lotions kept the skin smooth, and baths of asses' milk or foamy imported beer supposedly kept wrinkles at bay. Cucumber juice and vinegar removed freckles and other spots, which seemed to be a major concern (Pliny, *Natural History* 20.9, 20.125).

The satirists only emphasize downright appalling ingredients, the grease from wool, scum, crocodile dung, and ash (lead sulfide, a toxic substance, kept complexions fashionably pale although Romans were not aware of the dangers). Unlike the obscure chemical derivatives in our processed cosmetics, Roman concoctions seem so much the worse for having contents that were graphically explicit (Ovid, *Medicamina*, 209–34; Horace, *Epodes*, 12.9–11). Pliny also reports on a cosmetic method of taking revenge on a rival by killing a spotted lizard in her face cream to cause freckles (*Natural History* 29, 73)! We must conclude that some creams were truly muck, if the victim was not aware of the reptile or, at least, its demise in her ointment – getting freckles would have been the least of her worries. Cosmetics aided trickery, and women only saw each other as competition in Pliny's view. Rather than trivializing the beauty system, Pliny could have informed us that women shared recipes for their lotions and tonics, some of which may also have had medicinal purposes. Producing herbal remedies for healing was also women's work, for which we should expect knowledge passed down through families and among friends. Both cosmetics and natural medicine imply a community of interest, although the elite male occasionally suspected these practitioners of poisoning husbands or others (a far more serious crime than sabotaging an acquaintance's moisturizer).

It is not only women's faces that required intensive care. The pampered or painted face may have displaced attention from the hidden parts of the female anatomy. Medical treatments piped fumes in the nostrils or vagina to cure gynecological problems, and these also became part of the toilette. The poet Lucretius depicts the boudoir of a woman who "fumigates her wretched self with foul smells," while her maids flee in fits of giggles to get away from the odor of sulfur, urine, and dung being pumped up their mistress's body from below (*De Rerum Natura* 4.1174–1191, trans. A. Richlin). Lucretius takes up the satirists' point that a made-up face covers up a repulsive body and its interior; that is, the beauty business is a fraud.

Archaeology suggests that cosmetics were a thriving home industry supported by imports of precious ingredients. An excavation in the city of London turned up an extraordinary find, not simply a container for cosmetics but a jar of Roman face cream with its contents intact, apparently tightly sealed (http://www.bris.ac.uk/news/2004/590). The foundation of refined animal fat, starch, and tin created a pale, powdery texture when smoothed over the face. That it lasted over the centuries is a testament to the skills of Roman cosmeticians. We should not think of Roman women (not only elite matrons but also those with some resources) as being paralyzed by ideology, of believing the cant about their bodies being inferior and foul, rather they engaged in beauty regimens as activities that gave them some creative control over their appearances through the tried and true practices shared by their peers. Proper grooming and care suggested that well-kept matrons belonged to the higher status groups although there was the possibility that an actress could have passed for a respectable woman with the right look.

Makeup colored and highlighted women's features over the pale foundation. Rouge in the form of ochre, cinnabar or the sediment of red wine brightened cheeks and lips, and dark powders made from soot adorned eyelashes or lids. Saffron and ash could also be used as eye shadow. Although almost all of the marble portrait sculptures have lost the pigments originally applied to them, the painted mummy portraits of Roman Egypt offer glimpses of makeup (Figure 59). Endowed with a full complement of shadows and highlights to create a sense of depth, the portrait shows full pink lips with a silvery glint; the painted lips are bleached out to indicate light reflected off of their glossy surface. The subject's olive complexion is lighter on the cheeks and chin, where an

59. Detroit, The Detroit Museum of Arts, 25.2. The mid-second century portrait from Antinoopolis (see map) is made of encaustic (pigment mixed in melted wax) and gilt on a wood panel that covered the mummy's face. Some of the thick waxy paint was applied with a spatula or palette-knife, brushes were used in the other section. Note the lavish gold jewelry in relief.

ivory pigment with pink undertones may represent the subject's makeup in an application of foundation. The eyes received the lion's share of cosmetics in the form of black liner on the lower and upper lids, along with arcs of eye shadow in shades of pink to darker tones of lavender and violet in the crease beneath the heavy brows. We do not know if the subject was made-up like this everyday or, rather, if the cosmetics were reserved for formal occasions, such as her funeral and the portrait by which she is remembered.

The application of cosmetics required instruments for application. Long-handled spoons and chatelaines with scoops, nail cleaners, and tweezers have been found (Figure 60). Ceramic or glass perfume vials, make-up boxes, pestle-and-mortar sets (for grinding minerals into powders), and ointment jars litter many archaeological sites. More precious objects from the vanity table were occasionally buried with young women who died unmarried and, therefore, had no use for the finery of a bridal trousseau (see Minicia Marcella in Chapter 2). A silver mirror from a teenage girl's tomb south of Rome was found in the sarcophagus with the remains of the deceased (Figure 61). Graced with a mythological scene of a girl slipping from her brother's grasp as they race away from home on the back of a ram (the owner of the mirror would no doubt know that the girl, Helle, was doomed to fall into the water below that was then named the Hellespont in her honor, see map), the mirror alluded to the romantic world of myth with runaways and heroic adventures in far-off lands. The other, nondecorated side of the mirror was highly polished to reflect the girl's image.

60. London, Museum of London. The chatelaine would have been fixed to a woman's garments and traveled with her, rather like a modern compact, so that good grooming was always at hand.

61. Rome, Museo
Nazionale Romano, inv.
3941555. A silver mirror,
from tomb 2 from Vallerano
of the second century C.E.,
exhibits fine workmanship
with its back done in relief
representing the myth of
Phrixus and Helle, and
with its handle spirally
fluted. An inscription tells
the weight of the silver used
in this luxury object (most
mirrors were bronze).

Hair, as a woman's crowning glory, provided a rich field for styling
and adornment. In the early second century, the novelist Apuleius wrote
that a woman is not dressed if her hair is not properly fashioned (*Met.* 2.9)
(Figure 62). Hairstyles are thought to have followed the fashions of the
imperial womens, but Ovid states that everyday brings innumerable new
styles in the late first century B.C.E. (*Ars Amatoria* 3.149). We can observe
that female hairstyles move from prim arrangements of parted and plaited
hair in the late republic to more flamboyant piles of curls in the second
century C.E., but there is no clear linear evolution of styles in one direction. Hair is particularly interesting as a field of adornment because it can

be manipulated in many ways through cutting, curling, plaiting, wrapping, and dyeing (with "German juices" for lightening locks, Ovid, *Ars Amatoria*, 3.163–4). Curling irons were used to crimp hair and animal fats held stray locks in place. Hairdressers must have had advanced techniques to meet the demands of their mistresses, although the simple comb remained the most essential grooming instrument (Figure 63).

Roman women also added to their own supply of hair with wigs or hairpieces, and many of their high coiffures of the late first and second centuries C.E. depended on wigs. Poets inform readers where these could be purchased in the streets of Rome. Archaeology provides evidence of hairpieces in the form of a false braid or ponytail attached to a leather backing. Even portrait statues of matrons sported removable wigs, once

62. Yorkshire, Museum. A Head of auburn hair, from a woman's grave at York, fourth-century C.E. It has been coiled in a loose bun fixed by jet pins, which have delicate decoration on their tips.

63. London, British Museum. A third-century C.E. ivory comb with teeth on both sides is inscribed with the name of its owner and a message, "Modestina, farewell!" as if the object was speaking, sending its mistress out into the world after smoothing down her hair.

thought to have been updated with changes in hairstyles but more likely to have been depicted as indispensable items in grooming without which no respectable matron was properly done-up (Figure 64).

Moralists, of course, saw excess in the elaboration of coiffures, especially because a woman's head ought to be covered – literally, with a veil in the traditional manner, and metaphorically, by being modest and not carrying her head high. Juvenal comments on the transformative effects of big hair:

> So important is the business of beautification; so numerous are the tiers and storeys piled one upon another on her head! In front you would take her for an Andromache; she is not so tall behind: you would not think it was the same person. (*Satire* 6, 501–504, trans. P. Green)

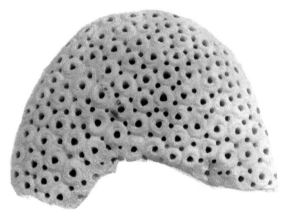

64. Ostia, Museo Ostiense, inv. 1931. A marble wig for a portrait statue in the Flavian style with its wreath or ringlets from the late first century C.E. See also the portrait of Julia Titi, Figure 88 in chapter four for this style.

The towering coiffure increases the woman's height and lends her the stature of the heroic Andromache of Greek myth, who remains beautiful and dignified under pressure. Again, the satirists charge women with deceit: the woman with the high hair appears to be disguised, as if the wig masked her identity. Coiffures molded in the form of tiaras or with bejeweled tiers of springing curls signaled sexual availability to staunch conservatives, but to other members of the equestrian and senatorial elite the hairstyles were deployed like regal headdresses (Figure 65). In the second century C.E., hair appears to have been shaped into turbans, crests, and crowns. That is, the hair with the aid of wigs took on the forms of exotic or stately headgear usually worn in religious or civic ceremonies. The coiffures, although attracting attention by their sumptuous styling, also covered the heads and real hair of women tucked under the wigs and, therefore, protected their modesty. Rather than creating an illusion of luxuriant sensuous hair, the wigs instead make an allusion to regalia of

65. London, British Museum, inv. 1925. Marble portrait bust of Claudia Olympias, mid-second century C.E. Its inscriptional plaque states that her freedman dedicated the bust.

66. London, British Museum. second century c.e.
HIP/Scala/Art Resource, N.Y., 179628. A hairpin made
of bone that is decorated with a bust of a woman wearing
a towering, many-tiered coiffure surmounted with
crenellations. Would this ample hairpin have held such a
coiffure in place?

honor, a feminine complement to political and military gear (Figure 66).
Male portraits in the mid–second century show longer hair worn in
masses of curls with beards; for the most part, the new styles with a softer
masculinity as seen in highly styled locks and beards (which signified the
Greek intellectual heritage) brought no outcry because of the Hadrianic
and Antonine endorsement of the look and Hellenism in general. Male
adornment, though, could have moral implications, particularly for the
political standing of civic leaders.

Feminine cultivation embraced both physical appearances and the
life of the mind. That making up and primping were not only seen as
frivolous can be attested by a funerary relief that commemorates a woman
in the process of being groomed with attributes of learning and culture.
A pair of stucco reliefs adorned a tomb in La Marsa near Carthage in
north Africa in the mid–second century (Figures 67 and 68). Probably
flanking the tomb entrance, the pair of reliefs are meant to be seen in

67 (Detail) and 68. Carthage, Museum, photo courtesy of Naomi Norman. A pair of stucco reliefs from La Marsa. Both stucco reliefs, from the mid–second century C.E., depict the same young woman, whose wig is similar to that seen in Figure 64.

69. Rome, Museo Nazionale Romano, 414060 and 414065. Necklace, second century C.E. The necklace has a crescent pendant consisting of green beryl beads strung with gold rod spacers on a string that has disintegrated.

sequence with one depicting the process of adornment in a scene of a slave braiding the hair of her mistress, while the other shows the woman alone, her coiffure in place, reading from a scroll, the ancient form of the book. Not intended to represent a cosmetic makeover, the scenes instead evoke the transformation of the woman as a process that uplifts both her locks and her mind. A cultivated woman needs to be both splendidly turned out (i.e., with every hair in place) and literate, if not intellectually engaged. Even the furniture, the chair with footstool, indicates quality, expense, and leisure.

Jewelry adorned hair, ears, necks, arms and fingers in relative profusion. Although the satirists saw the display of gold and silver as a waste of wealth, husbands and fathers seemed to have approved of jewelry as attested by the finds in tombs and, more significantly, the representations of gems on marble and painted portraits. A set of gold jewelry, composed of two necklaces, two armbands, three brooches, and six rings (Figure 69) was worn by the young woman buried with the silver mirror (Figure 61). That the jewelry was buried with the sixteen- or seventeen-year old suggests that she was unmarried, that is, without a daughter to whom she would leave her gems; jewelry formed part of the dowry the father would have been assembling, and the bridal trousseau became the finery for the tomb, as in the sad case of Minicia Marcella (see Chapter 2). The necklace features a pendant in the form of a lunar crescent, a fertility symbol seen throughout the empire and in the mummy portrait of Demo's daughter in Egypt (see Figure 41 in Chapter 2). The practice of burying fertility tokens with girls was a poignant expression of loss, not only of the girl's life but also of her children and their promise, now denied by death.

Most graves brought forth far fewer precious objects than those found in the affluent teenager's tomb because Romans found jewelry too valuable to be abandoned in graves, except in the cases of unmarried girls.

70. Cairo, Egyptian Museum, CG 33216, photo courtesy of Steve Vinson. The mummy, the "Golden Girl," exemplifies the fusion of different cultural traditions in Roman Egypt in the early second century C.E. The painted panel recalls the Roman tradition of portraying individuals, the custom of mummifying the body hearkens back to the traditions of Old Kingdom Egypt, also attested in the portrait's allusions to the Egyptian goddess Isis. The Greek language and culture of the Egyptian elite may be reflected in the allusion to the goddess Aphrodite (the Roman Venus) as seen in the girl's bare shoulder.

71. London, British Museum, EA 65346. HIP/Scala/Art Resource, N.Y., 179629. Later in date than the Golden Girl, this mummy portrait of ca. 161–192 C.E. exhibits colorful clothing, a green tunic with a gold stripe, which complements the color scheme of the ensemble of jewelry. It is curious that many of the women's tunics show brightly colored stripes, perhaps in playful imitation of the Roman custom of purple stripes marking the rank of elite male citizens.

The painted mummy portraits from Egypt, however, depict how women wore lavish ensembles of jewelry. An example is found in the mummy known as the "Golden Girl," from the early second century (Figure 70). The small size of the mummy indicates it was for a girl, whose painted portrait shows off expensive decoration in the jeweled headband, drop earrings, and several necklaces, some with emeralds and rubies, others with gold chains. The stucco mummy case is also adorned with gilt, gems, and colored glass in imitation of gemstones. We may suspect that the seven- to ten-year-old girl within the mummy case could not have stood up under the weight of this much gold and that her parents had her represented so richly to show that she was highly valued and, indeed, intensely mourned.

Another mummy portrait of a mature woman (Figure 71) demonstrates restraint in its adornment: a delicate gold wreath sits atop the head, the earrings consist of square emeralds with pearl drops, and the necklace has emeralds and a carnelian set in bold rectangular or oval mounts (the gilt has flaked off in sections here). Gold wreaths, which alluded to bridal finery for younger women, formed part of the funerary regalia for well-heeled women. The heavy gold mounts on the necklace indicate the expense involved in this type of jewelry, as opposed to the simpler technique of threading strands of beads on strings.

Regional variation is apparent in the adornment of women as represented in the funerary reliefs from Palmyra, a trading center strategically located on the routes across the Syrian desert (see map). One limestone relief (Figure 72) representing a matron exhibits bar earrings

72. Boston, Museum of Fine Arts, 22.659. A Palmyrene relief with a Greek inscription stating that it commemorates "Aththaia, daughter of Malchos." It dates to the late second century C.E. and is carved in limestone.

with pendant balls, familiar throughout the empire, and a necklace with the fertility symbol of the lunar crescent. Despite these familiar types of decoration, the softly folded turban with its finely worked band and studded straps at the sides of the head, the band of twisted metal holding the crescent pendant, and the prominent brooch with teardrop pendants distinguish this relief from other images of adorned women in the empire. Elements of standardization and variation are apparent in jewelry across the empire.

Jewelry, however, was too expensive to be left in the hands of women and had to be defined in legal terms by jurists since it constituted the wealth to be handed down from generation to generation. Women could leave legacies or bequests that their daughters be given their gems (or even state which necklaces with which they wished to be buried), and frequently these documents specify the disposition of every last piece of jewelry (note also the legal case of women robbed of their jewelry in the bathhouse, see Chapter 2). As family heirlooms and, especially, as objects that were passed from mother to daughter, jewels were invested with memories that could never be factored into their worth on the market. The prestige of wearing exquisite gems rested not only in their cost but in the possession of a family lineage that could provide a woman with such a heritage – on the one hand, there was the snob appeal of ancestry and, on the other, the emotional appeal of wearing a ring once worn by one's mother and grandmother. Many necklaces and bracelets look fairly uniform in forms and styles that were old-fashioned; it would be interesting to know if new jewelry was ever made in an antique style to affect the look of a cherished heirloom.

The Company of Women

Women had social lives that extended beyond their families; for some, the social rounds of visits were duties required by their husbands' positions, while others made the most of the company of their peers for their own well-being and amusement. Even if these activities merely occupied the time between more urgent tasks, the social calls, meetings, or entertaining entailed some planning or preparation, which required work (some of it done by slaves, messengers, maids, etc.). Even lower-status women took part; however, the wives of artisans or shopkeepers had less leisure time, if any at all, to unwind with their peers, trade gossip, and entertain one another after hours. A few traces remain of women's social life in the archaeological record and literary sources.

The social hostess appears in eighteenth- and nineteenth-century literature as a character who wields power, and in early modern Europe, sophisticated women held salons of intellectual and artistic figures. The hostess of the Roman banquet and the salon, however, does not figure prominently in many accounts (see Chapters 2 and 4, and the latter for exceptions among the imperial women – also Julia Domna, wife of the emperor Septimius Severus; r. 193–211), no doubt, because of the masculine dominance of the banquet and Roman uneasiness about intellectual pretensions (along with the relegation of most of what we would consider the arts to disreputable characters in the slums). Yet that we find hostesses planning parties in the isolated circumstances of a military camp on the frontier should allow us to consider that women managed this aspect of their lives probably more thoroughly than we have imagined.

Some women and children lived in the forts built along Hadrian's wall in England in the late first and second centuries C.E. (see map). The wives of officers settled in for long periods in what must have been isolated, dreary, and cold places lacking the urban amenities of home. Evidently, the ranking women had common ground and socialized among themselves, visiting surrounding forts to seek out their peers because there were few other women, especially of their status. A letter from Claudia Severa, a fort commander's wife, to Sulpicia Lepidina, wife of the senior officer at Vindolanda, invites her to a birthday party: "On the tenth of September, sister, for the day of the celebration of my birthday, I give you

73. London, British Museum, P 1986.10–1.64. HIP/Scala/Art Resource, N.Y., 179632. Wooden tablet with birthday invitation from Claudia Severa to Sulpicia Lepidina, 90–105 C.E. (*Tab. Vindol.* II 291). These thin wooden tablets functioned as letters, as did the papyri of Roman Egypt.

a warm invitation to make sure that you come to us, to make the day more enjoyable for me by your arrival, if you come. Give my greetings to your Cerialis. My Aelius and my little son send you their greetings. [the above was written by a scribe; the following in a second hand, no doubt, that of Claudia Severa herself] I shall expect you, sister. Farewell, sister, my dearest soul, as I hope to prosper and hail" (Figure 73). We need not imagine them only pouring tea and sharing little cakes because other letters itemize the varied larders of the forts (offering Celtic beer, imported Italian wine, fish sauce, pork fat). The letters hint at their deep affection for each other and suggest the ways in which they staved off boredom in these outposts.

An example of a house of the commanding officer can be seen in the aerial view of Housesteads Fort (Figure 74). The house, situated within the south gate, is built around a central open courtyard and possessed a kitchen with oven in one corner, while baths and a lavatory were added in the second century. The commanding officer and his family were to live in the style and comfort of home transferred to the military camp at the edge of the empire. Such a substantial dwelling required a staff to run it (some slaves may have accompanied the commander from Rome, while other household helpers may have been locals) and a vigilant mistress to watch over them. High living standards are also indicated in the personal effects found at the camps along Hadrian's wall, which include items of clothing such as a well-made woman's leather sandal (Figure 75).

Other women traveled with the army and stayed in the settlements that sprung up next to the camps and outside the walls of the forts (see Figure 74 for the inns and shops outside the walls visible as rows of rectangles). Soldiers below the rank of officers were forbidden to marry until a decree of 197 C.E. that allowed legal marriage and cohabitation; before this time, soldiers could always form relationships with women (either locals or those who had accompanied them from a previous posting) outside of marriage, and these women and children formed the entourage that followed the troops. The earlier ban on marriage may have resulted from concerns about maintaining the rigors of military life and the army's unwillingness to take responsibility for the wives and

74. Cambridge University Collection. Aerial view of Housesteads Fort, which is visible with its perimeter fortifications and regular division into quadrants within its rectangular plan.

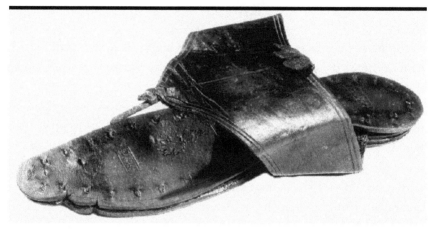

75. The Vindolanda Trust, Roman Army Museum; second century C.E. Woman's leather sandal stamped with the maker's name, L. Aebutius Thales, as if a brand name. The style is one that is still worn today with a thong next to the big toe and a wide band around the instep.

children of soldiers. Upon retirement (usually after twenty or twenty-five years or more of service), soldiers were granted citizenship (if they didn't already possess it) for themselves and their children, and the recognition of their marriages; some were granted land or given ample cash payments. Many chose to settle down in the vicinity of their old forts, where the bachelors would have made attractive suitors for local women (see Figure 36, the funerary relief of Flavia Augustina at York; her husband, Gaius Aeresius Saenus, retired to have his wife and two children die soon after).

The wives of soldiers and veterans found company in the markets and taverns of the towns where there was a wider culture with traveling shows of performers and musicians on market days. The army stimulated the economy of the towns that sprang to life outside the walls of its forts because of its steady demand for goods and the security it offered. Although lacking the breadth of opportunities and culture of a city, these towns were busy places with the activities of the troops and their dependents, the local merchants, and those traveling through to serve them. We should imagine women active in the society of the settlements since they were primarily responsible for their households (if common-law or, later, legal wives of soldiers) and free from the burdens of military schedules and duties. The mobility of troops and traders allowed for a cosmopolitan culture of many languages and backgrounds. The military culture of Rome was predominantly masculine, although it depended on women, from the officers' wives to the women shacked up with soldiers, along with the local girls working the taverns and others providing material support or labor.

That the army served as a vehicle for Romanization with its genius for molding men and providing instruction in basic Latin is well-known, but the itinerant merchants that moved across the empire from camp town to fort also made the world smaller and more familiar (Figure 76). They traveled long distances in wagons fitted with beds to sell goods that became standard throughout most of the empire. With them they brought stories of life elsewhere, news of current events, and the acquaintance of colleagues met along the way – some merchants' wives traveling with small children may have had greater need to seek assistance on the road (women acted as partners in the family business). If merchants made the same rounds seasonally, then the family would have been returning to friends year after year in the stops on their itinerary.

The wives of governors of provinces had official duties similar to those of contemporary wives of high state officials: they accompanied

76. Rome, Fototeca Unione. Alinari/Art Resource, N.Y., 113610. Relief in the Church of S. Maria Saal, second century C.E., Klagenfurt showing an elaborate covered wagon of the type that was used by itinerant traders or traveling families.

their husbands on some official visits or missions and served as hostesses at state receptions and dinners. It was considered normal for wives to accept petitions from provincial subjects, to receive them in the governor's house, and to make public appearances. Yet, the women's unofficial influence on their husbands could put them in compromising positions from unscrupulous provincials who thought they could gain favor with governors through their wives. The wife of the governor had to be involved with the most routine aspects of administration yet needed to distance herself from the most important (see Chapter 4 on the dilemma of politically engaged wives).

In Rome and Italy, there were ladies of leisure without official social duties who whiled away the hours in light entertainment. The younger Pliny tells of Ummidia Quadratilla who lived almost until the age of seventy-nine in good health in the early second century C.E. (*Epistles* 7.24). She had her own troupe of mime actors who played for her amusement and, we suppose, that of her friends. When the mimes performed in public, she became a benefactor and was applauded accordingly by the citizenry. She never allowed her grandson to watch the mimes until the public performance, and her vigilance and good sense in this was recognized by Pliny, who had supervised the boy's education. We may share Pliny's distaste for Ummidia Quadratilla's excess, for few women had the means to keep themselves amused with their own theatrical troupes. Yet, Pliny's anecdote gives a moralizing account of the differences between private and public life: the mime troupe, praised as a gift to her fellow citizens when they performed in public, is an overindulgence when kept at home for her own entertainment. Pliny also notes that the elderly woman played board games to pass the time, another frivolous activity deemed unsuitable for her grandson to watch; instead of imagining Ummidia Quadratilla closeted away with her actors and checkerboard, we should think of her as the hostess of grand dinners in which her troupe played between courses and the organizer of more modest gatherings in which the women shared their news, relaxed and, perhaps, played games.

Matronae Doctae

Girls were educated in some elite families because they were expected to be informed companions of husbands in the higher echelons of political service or simply because it was believed that girls benefited from some polish that would allow them to get on, or even stand out, in their brilliant social circles (see Chapter 2). Women were literate, wrote poetry, and discussed philosophy as *matronae doctae*, learned women (however, in far fewer numbers than in contemporary Western societies). Satirists, as usual, mocked their intellectual interests as the amateurish pretensions of rich and vain women. Poetry and philosophy did not comprise occupations, that is, ways of making a living for women. Teachers tended to be male, even on the grammar school level. There may be a few exceptions, and one is depicted in a mummy portrait inscribed in Greek, "Hermione Grammatike," that is, "Hermione, teacher of Greek grammar" (Figure 77). Some scholars have interpreted the inscription as merely referring to Hermione's literacy, but others have noted that teachers of Greek in Roman Egypt were highly respected for their efforts in preserving Hellenic traditions and were honored for their accomplishments, thus, the title, "grammatike" given to the deceased teacher. Mummies with portraits provide extraordinary opportunities for scientists and archaeologists to match the physical remains of the deceased with the features of the painted portrait: X-rays revealed that Hermione died between the ages of sixteen and twenty-five and had delicate features and good teeth, a sign of general well-being and care, which is matched by the looks of the portrait. Furthermore, the mummy wrappings, consisting of six to eight layers of linen folded in an intricate rhomboid pattern, indicate that a considerable sum was spent on Hermione's mummy and burial. Evidently a teacher in provincial Egypt merited a fine burial as a highly regarded professional mourned by her family, colleagues, and students.

In the markets and shops of Rome, literate women put their skills to work (Figure 78). The relief, which probably once decorated a tomb

77. Cambridge, Girton College. The mummy of Hermione Grammatike. The portrait is painted on the linen wrapping of the mummy and depicts a young woman with a mid–first century C.E. hairstyle and prim pearl earrings. Some have thought her demure appearance appropriate for a schoolteacher!

façade, depicts a shop with the butcher at work at the right, and a woman writing on wax tablets on the left. The scene sets forth the division of labor: the woman appears to be managing the shop by working on the accounts, while the butcher is shown cutting the meat. Most of the relief is given over to a description of the butcher's shop with its hanging cuts of pork, scales, and bucket collecting slops below. The seated woman faces the butcher's workspace; yet, it is not likely that such a stately armchair and footstool actually graced the shop. The woman's role was elevated by the depiction of expensive furniture and props, usually found in representations of goddesses or mythological figures. The practical application of learning is placed on a pedestal here, both literally and figuratively, and the woman looks more like the *matrona docta*, an ideal that seems to have resonated even among some members of the lower social orders. If we imagine that the butcher and his accountant were husband

and wife (there is no inscription to inform us of their relationship), then the scene may have represented a family business.

Saleswomen

Women worked outside of the home – many, both slaves and freed-women, worked in other women's houses, as we have seen in the example of wet nurses and midwives, as well as with the domestic staff. Other women of the lower social orders were tradeswomen or artisans as attested by epitaphs – a browse through the corpus of Latin inscriptions turns up a female dealer in grains, a mosaic worker, and perfumer, among many others (*CIL* 6. 9683; 5.7044; 6.10006). Freeborn girls completed apprenticeships in crafts or trades less frequently than slave girls did. Women worked (some alongside their husbands) in a wide range of occupations in small businesses, retail shops, or workshops producing goods. Of all of these, saleswomen are represented in a number of reliefs from Italy and the provinces that depict scenes of the commercial life of stalls and shops. Women without other means of support found a living selling produce or

78. Dresden, Staatliche Kunstsammlungen, inv. ZV 44. Alinari/Art Resource, N.Y., 105877. The relief of the butcher's shop can be dated to the mid–second century by the woman's hairstyle with braids wrapped to form a turban, which appears to be rather formal for the setting.

79. Ostia, Museo Ostiense, inv. 198. Erich Lessing/Art Resource, N.Y., 14792. The relief of the greengrocer, late second century C.E. Note the frontality of the composition and the clarity of the produce for sale, design elements characteristic of signs and advertising. See map for Ostia.

handmade goods, jobs that put them in the public eye but marked them off as women of low morals or easy virtue, according to the elite point of view. The only records of their lives are epitaphs and reliefs, most of which decorated their tombs, while others may have served as shop signs of the most prosperous businesswomen. The greengrocers and hawkers of poultry were unworthy of consideration and, therefore, invisible to most of the poets and historians whose texts form the standard accounts of Roman life.

A second-century relief of a greengrocer from Ostia, the port of Rome, depicts a stall formed by a trestle table atop sawhorses and piled high with baskets of various vegetables for sale (Figure 79). Made in the typical style of workers' scenes, the plaque is carved in low relief with emphasis on linear detail in the depiction in the varieties of vegetables for sale (garlic, cauliflower, zucchini), while the half-figure of the greengrocer behind the table shows the simplified and rough forms of a rounded face with hair pulled back and a body clothed in a loose tunic and mantle. Lacking the individualized facial features of a portrait, the figure instead appeals with a gesture that signals speech with the two little fingers in a closed position with the others extended on the oversized hand. The grocer is shown pointing to her goods and addressing a potential customer in the characteristic tactic of the "hard sell," long familiar to us from advertising and the media as a valued technique to get attention in a crowded, noisy market. It is interesting that the greengrocer, lacking the stately props and elegant hairstyle of the woman in the butcher shop (Figure 78), is identified by the quality of her goods and her actions, which show her to have the mettle of a seasoned saleswoman.

Another second-century relief of a saleswoman shows a more densely populated scene of market life (Figure 80). The woman behind the counter is selling poultry and rabbits, the ears of the latter are seen poking out of their cages on the lower right. Two monkeys sitting on the counter above are not for sale but, rather, probably attracted a crowd out of curiosity and may have performed for their amusement. The Roman market had a carnival atmosphere of an Asian bazaar with exotic and wondrous things to see, and, no doubt, this vendor would have been remembered for the display of the monkeys, if not for her tasty chickens. The saleswoman is shown handing objects that may be eggplants or round loaves of bread to a customer, a small fellow to the left of the

80. Ostia, Museo Ostiense, inv. 134. Erich Lessing/Art Resource, N.Y., 41715. The relief of the poultry vendor, late second century c.e. The large snail in the background may have been a brand or logo of the business and, thus, represents a sign.

counter. That this business seems well-established is also attested by the presence of an assistant to the left of the saleswoman who watches the transaction. The other half of the relief is given over to a representation of two male figures in cloaks: one gestures broadly, while the other seems to be holding a recent purchase, a rabbit or chicken (there is also poultry strung up from a frame in the background). In contrast to the concentrated focus of the greengrocer's relief, this scene buzzes with activity and lively exchanges from the three pairs: the male bystanders, the saleswoman and customer, and the monkeys, whose lackadaisical attention seems to drift to what lies outside of the frame.

The saleswomen in both reliefs are commemorated in ways that summon the conventional or cherished notions about getting and spending in the marketplace. The one relief has the greengrocer hawking her wares directly to the viewer who stands in for the customer, while the other has the vendor engaging in a charming vignette of a colorful market scene. Despite their detailed depiction of the trestle tables, hampers, and animal cages, the scenes do not give a realistic representation of the women's work – there is no interest in showing them acquiring their goods, stacking, cleaning, or plucking them. What we see is the most public and characteristic activity of the women in their stalls appealing to passersby. This is also the part of the job that made the women appear disreputable and degraded to elite men, who saw them as aggressive, shameless, and surely willing to sell their bodies as easily as they would hand over a head of garlic. It is striking that the reliefs celebrate the qualities that ensured the saleswomen's success and also demonstrated their marked difference from the modest and demure matrons of the grand houses. The imagery captures a world apart from the polite society of most of the literary sources and, at the same time, allows for the clichés of that world to flourish.

CHAPTER 4

PUBLIC LIFE

Roman women took part in public life to a greater degree than might be expected of ancient societies. Their role in politics must be qualified, however, to acknowledge that their access depended on the status of their fathers or husbands and that their activities and influence were often indirect, behind the scenes. Without a constitutional role in the political system, women reacted *en masse* in protest against unjust conditions in the republic (see Chapter 1), and a few prominent women wielded considerable authority in the empire because of family ties, especially in the tangled skein of multiple marriages, adoptions, and the dynastic strategies of Augustus and his heirs. Ambitious aristocratic women had no choice but to work their way through men, which has given rise to the clichés of the schemer, the poisoner, and the ungovernable matron who craves power. This chapter tests the cliché against biographical sketches of a several women who figured as matriarchs, political wives, or imperial women.

The chapter then turns to the sphere of religion in which women fully participated as worshipers and priestesses. The accounts of the origins and rituals of cults give evidence of the collective activities of mostly anonymous women whose lives were punctuated by the religious calendar with its regular rounds of processions and offerings; these events gave these women a public life, that is, activities and influence beyond their households. Furthermore, many of the cults defined female roles and prescribed norms of behavior, often linking the cult or its deity to the mythical foundations of Rome – in this way, religion supported the state and served its political and military goals. Men dominated religious life, which overlapped the political sphere (for Romans, the sacred and secular were virtually indistinguishable). Some cults excluded women, although there were female priests of state cults. Women's participation in the bewilderingly rich and varied menu of cults that constituted Roman religion was in no way marginal. In fact, many cults acknowledged that wives and mothers were central to the well-being of Rome. It should be noted, however, that most of women's duties and obligations were in the private or domestic sphere (although the boundaries between private and public were blurry).

We begin with women who figured in the course of history, who witnessed or participated (if only in supporting domestic roles although some broke through the stereotype) in the major events of the republic and empire. The ancient sources recorded their names only to praise or blame them; the written accounts neither offer nuanced judgments nor information on aspects that seem important to us, such as the motivation or psychology of the subjects. The authors of the primary sources do not reveal any conflicts of interest in their highly biased reports (nor would it have occurred to them to do so), and they seem to be grappling with ways to account for powerful, authoritative matrons, a contradiction in terms for a society in which a good woman was to be modest, dutiful, and demure. In the following biographical sketches, a fine line is drawn between women who merit praise because of their political skills and others who are held in contempt because of their overarching ambition, which was considered unnatural in women. The personalities of Livia or the younger Agrippina, for example, do not emerge from these documents or images, which elevate the former as the first lady of the Roman empire and relegate the latter to the degraded status of a conniving stage mother and deserving victim of her unbalanced son. The tendency was to cast the women as models, even though their lives were unique and not usually applicable in an inspirational or uplifting manner to womankind. Alternatively, they were vilified as monsters, cautionary examples of women whose refusal to stay in their place made them seem less than human.

The Republic: Cornelia and Fulvia

Cornelia (ca. 180–105? B.C.E.), known as the mother of the Gracchi, has achieved legendary status in Roman history. She is extolled because of her impeccable bloodlines and credentials as the daughter of Scipio Africanus, the general who defeated Hannibal in 202 B.C.E., and as the wife of Tiberius Sempronius Gracchus, another scion of a noble clan who had served as consul in 177 and 163. Cornelia witnessed the tumultuous events of the midyears of the republic with an insider's perspective through her relationships with the leading men. Near the end of her days, living in retirement on the Italian southern coast, she continued to regale visitors with her recollections of her father's life, so cherished were the memories of his heroic feats among the members of the intellectual set who frequented her establishment. Her husband also took on the dimensions of a monumental figure: Tiberius Sempronius Gracchus, despite his political resumé, was respected more for his virtues than his honors.

Cornelia reflected the glory of her husband and father. In keeping with elite practices, her marriage was arranged to form an alliance between two illustrious lines. Sempronius Gracchus (born ca. 215) was also older than his wife, as was typical, but legend has it that he brought on his own death: by following a portent that required him to sacrifice his own life, he ensured that his wife would live (Cicero, *De divinatione* 1.36). For this ultimate sacrifice, Sempronius merited the highest honors as an example of piety. His actions were not in vain, as Plutarch informs us about Cornelia's subsequent life:

> She took upon herself the burden of her children and the managing of her patrimony and proved to be so wise, so full of motherly love and so noble of character that it would seem Tiberius has made no mistake when he chose to die in place of such a woman. (Plutarch, *Tiberius Gracchus* 1.6, trans. A. H. Clough)

There are aspects of her life that coincide with those of women of less illustrious lineages: her rather early widowhood that left her to raise her twelve children, although only three survived to adulthood. Her wealth provided some relief from this unfortunate situation, although some sources suggest that the family fortune may have been in decline. In a well-known anecdote, Cornelia, after having been shown an ostentatious matron's finery, replied that her sons were *her jewels* (Valerius Maximus, 4.4.1). Set against the backdrop of the sumptuary laws of the second century B.C.E. (see Chapter 1) in which the wealth of women and its display were at issue, this anecdote defines Cornelia as a traditional matron, that is, the *univira*, married only once and devoted to her family, rather than one who prefers to go about the city all decked out and riding in a gleaming or gaudy carriage.

Cornelia distinguished herself in raising and educating her sons above all else. She selected the tutors of her sons, Tiberius and Gaius, who "though they were without dispute in natural endowments and dispositions the first among the Romans of the time, yet they seemed to owe their virtues ever more to their education than their birth" (Plutarch, *Tiberius Gracchus* 7, trans. A. H. Clough). The quality of the Gracchi's education and their thorough knowledge of Greek was attributed to their mother's care and diligence in seeking out the best scholars; yet, Cornelia's own cosmopolitan upbringing among learned men and intellectuals must have prepared her for this. In this aspect, she resembles elite women of the highest ranks who directly supervised their children's education (and managed households of the size and complexity of small firms; see Chapter 3).

Yet, Cornelia tests our notions of the traditional matron in several ways: she was a learned woman, fluent in Greek and competent in rhetoric, subjects of the curriculum that were taught to elite youths but not their prospective wives. Upon reading some of Cornelia's correspondence, Cicero remarked "that he understood why it was said that her sons 'had been raised in eloquence rather than in their mother's womb'," (Cicero, *Brutus* 211, trans. G. L. Hendrickson). Furthermore, fragments of letters that Cornelia may have written reveal refinement and sophistication in the persuasive arts – even if forged as many believe, the letters indicate the importance of her literary culture and the high esteem it brought her. Furthermore, the subject of a suspect letter, her son Gaius' land reforms, suggests an interests in politics (admittedly, the nature of the evidence invites caution). That Gaius refers to her in his speeches (extant in fragments) also reflects her wide renown and respect. Cornelia's public role, bestowed on her through both her bloodlines and her innate qualities may have differed in degree, if not in kind, from that of other elite matrons in the republic.

Lastly, an extraordinary honor was accorded Cornelia: a bronze statue was erected in a public portico in Rome in ca. 100 B.C.E. or, perhaps, slightly later (Figure 81). Inscribed, "Cornelia, daughter of Africanus, the mother of the Gracchi," the statue attests to her fame, and her standing as a public figure. Only a few exceptional women in the republic broke into the prestigious arena of acclaim evinced by the granting of a public statue (see Chapter 1). The statue of Cornelia depicts the matron in a seated pose, also characteristic of goddesses represented seated or enthroned with an air of stately dignity. The statue is preserved only through a later copy representing the mother of the emperor Constantine in the late empire; obviously, this type remained popular for the commemoration of good women through the course of centuries. Worthy of honor, Cornelia served as a model for matrons (especially under Augustus, whose program of moral reform made use of Cornelia's legendary status; see later), and her characterization as the chaste widow and devoted mother complemented her cultivated *persona* and intellectual leanings. Although feminine modesty and rarefied interests may seem to clash, they apparently resided comfortably within the complex character of Cornelia, a woman who also attracted an offer of marriage from King Ptolemy of Egypt after she had been widowed. Naturally, she turned him down.

A woman who intervened in the political or military spheres risked her reputation because (it was thought) such women took action not merely to be like men but to do the unthinkable – to rule them. One woman labeled as such was Fulvia (d. 40 B.C.E.), born into a noble house and married three times, the third and final time to Mark Antony during the volatile years of civil war at the end of the republic. The number of marriages was typical for an elite woman, especially for one from an old consular family with great wealth. Her first two marriages to Clodius and Curio established her family's alliance with the *populares,* the progressive party in republican politics associated with Julius Caesar. For this she attracted the enmity of Cicero who spared no opportunity to slander her; indeed, it is difficult to glimpse Fulvia without the glare of scandal's spotlight that Cicero focused on her.

81. Rome, Captitoline Museums, inv. 496. Scala/Art Resource, N.Y., 84909. Statue of Helena, mother of the emperor Constantine, early fourth century C.E., that may copy the esteemed type of the seated statue of Cornelia.

The sources gloss over her life as a wife and mother, and focus on the events during the civil war after Julius Caesar's assassination in 44 B.C.E. when Mark Antony, Caesar's ally, and Octavian, Caesar's adopted son and grandnephew (who took the title of Augustus in 27 B.C.E.), joined forces to avenge Caesar's assassination. Plutarch states that Fulvia was not a woman "of humble thoughts, content to spin wool and tidy the house; she was not satisfied with dominating her husband in private but wanted to dominate him as a magistrate and have command over him while he commanded legions (*Antony* 10.5, trans. A. H. Clough)." In this reasoning, a woman in control denotes a household and the state spinning out of control. During the proscription of 43 B.C.E. in which Caesar's and Antony's enemies were hunted down and killed, Fulvia allegedly defiled the decapitated head of Cicero. In the Perusian War of 41 B.C.E., it is reported that Fulvia took charge since Antony was in Egypt and instigated a disastrous conflict over land for veterans, which turned into a war pitting Antony's and Octavian's forces against each other. She donned military gear, including a sword in an early example of cross-dressing, which created a stir. She seems to have been represented on coins (minted outside of Rome) as a personification of victory in the form of a winged feminine bust. Amid conflicting charges of shrewdness, boldness, and foolhardiness, Fulvia recedes from view. The propaganda that portrays her as a bloodthirsty female general has less to do with Fulvia than with the anxieties aroused by a woman in her position. That she died suddenly soon after this, and was replaced in Antony's affections by his fourth wife, Octavia, and then by his lover, Cleopatra VII, did not help clear her name.

The Empire: Livia and the Agrippinas, Boudicca, Julia Titi, Sabina, and the Younger Faustina

When Octavian was left as the sole ruler of Rome in 31 B.C.E. after the battle of Actium, in which he defeated Mark Antony and Cleopatra, he began to restructure the government: he preferred the title of Augustus for himself to avoid the taint of the monarchy or dictatorship, he controlled membership in the senate and brought in new men from the provinces to reinvigorate its ranks, and he also gave capable equestrians more extensive roles in a revamped imperial bureaucracy and even prosperous freedmen a stake in the empire with priesthoods in cults (the *Augustales*). Augustus was careful to evoke the spirit of the republic to allay the fears of conservatives, but in reality, the republic had long been forsaken for a system in which the power was concentrated in his own hands.

Augustus's wife and first lady of the empire, Livia (58 B.C.E.–29 C.E.), maintained a unique position. He had divorced his previous wife, with whom he had one daughter, Julia, after he met Livia at a dinner party and was immediately taken by her. Livia had been married to Tiberius

Claudius Nero with whom she had one son, Tiberius, and was pregnant with another, Drusus, at the time. T. Claudius Nero graciously divorced his wife so that she could marry Octavian in 38 B.C.E. His compliance was, no doubt, secured by Octavian's political clout, the repercussions of which were well known to Livia. She had to flee to Greece in 40 B.C.E. when T. Claudius Nero was proscribed by Octavian, and she knew that her father committed suicide after supporting Brutus and Cassius, the murderers of Julius Caesar, at the battle of Philippi in 42 B.C.E. There is no better evidence of the Augustan period as one of transformation at the best, or of smoke and mirrors at worst, than in Livia's career: she was raised as an enemy of Octavian and wound up as his wife. Marriage to Livia also gave Octavian a valuable connection to one of Rome's oldest aristocratic lineages, regardless of their current position. Men, as well as women, gained prestige and status by marrying well.

The political role that Livia played in the Augustan court was partly informal because of the trust she inspired in her husband, and partly official, as a result of the number of honors that accrued to her and worked to compound her prominence and authority. The ancient sources had difficulty defining Livia: for some, she remained the industrious, old-fashioned matron weaving the wool for Augustus's togas, while others revert to the other stereotype of the woman scheming behind the throne (and poisoning Augustus's heirs to clear the way for her son Tiberius to become emperor). The wife of the first citizen assumed a position that had to be cobbled together from various spheres of activity. She engaged in religious activities and charity work as a matter of course. Like influential men and women throughout the empire, she served in more overtly political roles as a patron and builder. In political matters, she advised Augustus, who had copies of court documents brought to her quarters. It has been pointed out that Livia's sphere of influence ranged from the domestic and maternal to the civic and bureaucratic, with emphasis along the fault line where the two sectors merged, such as in religion. It comes as no surprise, then, that contemporary observers and later historians could not characterize her position without facing down its contradictions.

82. Copenhagen, Ny
Carlsberg Glyptotek,
inv. 1444. Portrait of Livia,
4–14 C.E., erected in an
amphitheater, along with
busts of Augustus and
Tiberius, to honor the
imperial family in a town in
the Fayum, Egypt.

Previously, Augustus had enabled Livia and his sister Octavia
(although the latter's marriage to Mark Antony already gave her prominence) to take the public stage in 35 B.C.E. through a special grant of
sacrosanctity. This allowed the two honored women to be financially
independent (released from a guardian's supervision); furthermore, the
grant allowed them special protection for their actions, a remarkable step
because it was associated with the privileges of public office and political
duties. Augustus thus expected them to act independently and empowered them to do so. That statues of Livia and Octavia were erected to
commemorate this novel step also suggests how closely the two women
approached the male model of the public figure in matters of commemoration and display (Figure 82). The remarkable number of portrait statues
of Livia attested to her appeal not only as the emperor's wife but as a

public figure in her own right. The portraits adhere to certain standards in uniformly representing Livia as a youthful woman with emphatically symmetrical features – the oval face, large almond-shaped eyes, the finely chiseled nose, small mouth and chin – that impress the viewer with their perfection. We do not know what Livia looked like, but the high degree of stylization in the simplified and regular features of the portraits suggest that the court artists improved on nature. Eminently recognizable, Livia's portraits project an image of pristine beauty, innate goodness, and a sense of steadfastness to principle. Both Livia's and Augustus's portraits remain consistently youthful throughout his reign, despite the aging of their subjects; although Livia's career was extended after Augustus's death, as she was the mother of the succeeding emperor, Tiberius, her later images barely suggest a more matronly appearance. The south frieze of the Ara Pacis (Figure 83) shows the predilection for idealized forms in the elegantly carved figures of Livia, her son-in-law Agrippa, and a young boy (either her grandson Gaius or a foreign prince, son of a client king) among the members of the imperial court in procession. Amid the

83. DAI, Rome, 72.2403. Scala/Art Resource, N.Y., 4579. The Ara Pacis, 13–9 B.C.E., section of the south frieze.

reliefs representing the legendary founders of Rome, the imperial family is given pride of place in the frieze of the Ara Pacis, which was dedicated on her birthday. In the same frieze, children are depicted tugging on their parents' garments or hands; the personification of the Italian land Tellus Italia balances two infants on her lap in the panel on the east end (see Figure 14 in Chapter 1), and the decorative vine scrolls below allude to a golden age of a well-ordered world in bloom and multiplying. The imagery of regeneration in the landscape and the close-knit family groups dovetail nicely with Augustus's marriage laws and his program of moral reform. Augustus and Livia presided over the rebirth of imperial society as depicted in the reliefs of the Ara Pacis. Despite Augustus's overarching vision for the revival of the Roman family, Livia's position as matriarch was not diminished by the fact that she did not bear Augustus children, especially an heir.

Among Livia's other privileges, the right to ride in a *carpentum*, a two-wheeled, horse-drawn vehicle, not only provided transportation for her rounds in the city but also may have recalled the spectacle of women of the early republic. Their elaborately ornamented vehicles provided not only mobility but status – such ostentatious displays incurred strict regulation in the republic. Augustus permitted Livia to escape from many constrictions in the course of the duties that defined her new role. She took the public stage as a patron of certain social groups and as a sponsor of worthy endeavors. Rome figured in Livia's plans as she embarked on building projects, typically the domain of male politicians or dynasts keen to leave their mark on the city. Temples, founded or restored, and buildings of public utility, such as porticoes and markets, merited Livia's sponsorship and linked her name with venerable sites in the city of Rome.

This privilege granted early in Livia's career as first lady foreshadows her later religious roles. She assumed priesthoods in various cults, was the sponsor of many offerings and festivals in honor of Augustus and, finally, was deified in 41 C.E. after her death (Figure 84). Her prominence in the sacred sphere is traditional except for the wide range of her activities. Elite matrons had long served as priestesses for various

84. Copenhagen, Ny Carlsberg Glypotek, inv. 1643. Portrait statue of Livia as Fortuna from Pozzuoli, Italy, mid–first century C.E. The statue represents Livia in a divine guise with the attribute of the cornucopia identifying her with the personification of fortune. This type of statuary became popular for commemorations of citizens – see a Roman matron represented as Venus in Figure 99 and a girl as Diana in Figure 101.

cults with the only requirement being their sterling reputations and their means to fund offerings and festivals; being a priestess in ancient Rome did not require a woman to be celibate or unmarried (with the exception of the Vestal Virgins; see "Religious Duties and Sacred Vows") – in fact, we may think of Roman priestesses (with some adjustments) as today's society women serving on the boards of civic groups or charitable organizations and making appearances at their benefits and galas. Livia's role as priestess thus complemented her exceptional position at the apex of Roman society. Her great wealth brought her priesthoods in provincial cities who honored her in hope of special dispensation or simply for the pleasure of making the appropriate gesture to the imperial house. In this way and others, she became a patron of peoples across the empire, and, on the rare occasion, intervened in imperial politics on their behalf. An inscription from Spain, recently recovered, indicates that Livia succeeded in obtaining a petition for her friend Plancina in a treason trial – clearly, she had influence in the senate (the Senatus Consultum de Cn. Pisone Patre; see http://muse.jhu.edu/journals/american_journal_of_philology/v120/1 . . .).

With Augustus's death in 14 C.E., Livia performed her duties as widow in an exemplary fashion, staying at his funeral pyre for days on end (Figure 85). Livia's display of grief was both typical and extreme in that women were responsible for washing the bodies of their loved ones and caring for their remains until they were interred; yet, few pursued their duty so thoroughly and unrelentingly. Her husband's will ensured that she was adopted as Augustus's daughter and renamed "Julia Augusta," a move not to diminish her role but to give her membership in the dynasty as kin and bestow on her a title equivalent to Augustus's in terms of prestige. She also gained a new priesthood in the cult of *Divus Augustus*, that is, of the god Augustus in the imperial cult that became important in the Italian towns and provinces, as well as in Rome. As keeper of the flame of Augustus's legacy, Livia served as priestess in his cult and no one needed to be reminded that she was now also descended from divinity. Her status changed from wife of the emperor to mother of the emperor with the accession of her son Tiberius to the throne (r. 14–37 C.E.), a development that reflected her tireless efforts to promote her son. She continued many of her honorary functions and received some new ones, but the most important, the title of *mater patriae*, mother of the country, was vetoed by Tiberius. Rather than attributing this to conflict between mother and son, we should be aware of the peculiarities of Livia's position in the Roman state and the burdens placed on her son, who owed his success to her but needed to establish his own regime. Livia continued in her role as the leading woman in the imperial court until her death in 29 but was not made a goddess, *Diva Augusta*, until 41 when Claudius, her grandson, became emperor.

What did it mean to become a goddess? The term *diva* now refers to a star who has reached the highest pinnacle of achievement in the field of the arts and entertainment with an aura of celebrity, wealth, and glamour. To the Romans it was literally a title indicating the highest honor a mortal could achieve and was bound up with the state religion that gave divine

85. Vienna, Kunsthistorisches Museum, IX A 95. The gemstone depicts Livia as a priestess of the deified Augustus, contemplating a bust of Augustus, after 14 C.E. Livia's image is crafted to evoke several goddesses: the crown evokes Fortuna, the shield represents the lions of Cybele (an eastern goddess imported to Rome), the poppies Ceres (the goddess of the flowering earth), and the slipping garment Venus.

sanction to the emperor and his policies. In the hierarchical society of Rome with its obsession with rank, it merited as the ultimate dignity that elevated the holder above one's peers and demanded the highest respect. As with many aspects of official life, the significance of titles and honors seems to reflect the brilliant displays of imperial ceremony or court pageantry – what we may have once called rituals empty of content – but now are seen to be invested with a symbolism of wider importance. Although it is difficult to reconstruct what the Romans believed, we may consider that becoming a goddess meant being inducted into the pantheon, if not of the divinities of Mt. Olympus than that of the ancestors of Augustus. The venerable ancestors included Venus and Mars through the weaving together of the foundation myths of Aeneas and Romulus. Virgil's epic, the *Aeneid*, which was written in the Augustan age in the twenties B.C.E., recounts the story of Aeneas, the hero who gradually comes around to his divine mission to found Rome after a humble beginning as a refugee from burning Troy (also depicted in a relief panel of the Ara Pacis). As Rome's national epic, the *Aeneid* gives Augustan Rome deep roots in the Hellenic world and divine approval of its imperial designs, as well as a sense of the historic destiny of Aeneas and his line. With Augustus and Livia joining their illustrious ancestors in the heavens, the first dynasty of Rome took part in the mythology of Rome. Evidence of the deification of Livia abounds in inscriptions with this title and statuary with divine motifs (Figures 84 and 85). Yet, we may still feel some uneasiness as we wonder what it was to become a goddess: we are left with the honorary title that alludes to nothing short of a miraculous change in form, which was symbolized at imperial funerals by releasing an eagle to soar upward; what Romans thought of this is open to question (and there were the inevitable jokes), but one result of deification was to create a vast gulf between the immortalized and her subjects.

The dynasty established by Augustus and Livia called the Julio-Claudians (a term devised by modern scholars) – taking its name from *Julius* Caesar, Augustus's adopted father, and Tiberius *Claudius* Nero, Livia's first husband and Tiberius's father, and ruling Rome from 31 B.C.E.–68 C.E. – was plagued by dominant women, according to historians. Prominent among them are the Agrippinas, mother and daughter designated as the elder and younger. Agrippina the elder (14/13 B.C.E.–33 C.E.) was the granddaughter of Augustus from his daughter, Julia, and wife of Germanicus, Livia's grandson. The women of this generation accompanied their husbands when they served abroad, rather than remaining in Rome as women did in the republic. This new role for wives of officials inevitably changed or complicated their lives, adding responsibilities and offering new experiences, often in harsh conditions and alien landscapes. Not the first woman to go abroad, the elder Agrippina was able to take advantage of a shift in policy, the subject of a senatorial debate in 20 C.E. Blessed with such a stellar lineage, Agrippina gained a reputation for being fierce and assertive when she accompanied her husband on military campaigns in Germany: she

86. New Haven, Yale University Art Gallery, inv. 12663. Bronze coin, sestertius, of Agrippina I, 37–38 C.E., Rome. The reverse of the coin depicts a *carpentum*, a luxurious carriage used by aristocratic matrons, although this carriage transported the urn with Agrippina's ashes and brought them to their final resting place. The coin contains a legend: S.P. Q. R. MEMORIAE AGRIPPINAE "The Senate and People of Rome dedicated it to the Memory of Agrippina."

appeared in the field with her young son Caligula dressed as a soldier to win sympathy from troops engaged in mutiny, and she also exercised decisive leadership and authority to stop troops from demolishing a bridge that would have trapped the Roman forces on the other side of the Rhine in 15 C.E. What we may interpret as quick-witted and shrewd responses to threats (which left her husband Germanicus stymied) were seen by others as unsavory displays of feminine arrogance because heroism was unbecoming to women. Although Agrippina was praised for her courage, the emperor Tiberius found a woman in the role of a military commander to be an unnatural and dangerous precedent. Like most women, Agrippina's life was shaped by the careers of her male relatives, and in her case, her identity as Augustus's only living descendant brought her enormous respect and popularity with the public (Figure 86).

Agrippina's role as a survivor of illustrious men emerged in her marriage as well: her husband's early death at the age of thirty four in 19 C.E. left her with great reservoirs of public sympathy. Germanicus was beloved by the Roman people – all the more so because he didn't live to achieve full glory – and in death his glowing memory burnished the image of his widow. Public opinion followed her to the extent that a party or faction formed around her and her eldest son. At the very least, Tiberius resented Agrippina's popularity, and then he grew to see her as a threat with the encouragement of his advisor. Furthermore, the elder Agrippina had a sharp mind and well-developed sense of integrity – one might call it entitlement, as she had allegedly taunted Tiberius with the reminder that she was a blood relation of Augustus (thus calling into question Tiberius's claim to the succession; Tacitus, *Annals* 4. 52–53). After the death of Livia, her protector, Agrippina's outspokenness and lack of tact (according to Tacitus, who demonized the Julio-Claudian women) led to her denouncement and banishment to an island off the coast of southern Italy in 29 C.E.

Her daughter, the younger Agrippina (15–59 C.E.), exemplifies the full flowering of the type of the *imperatrix*, the female commander. The mother may have dabbled at playing field general, but the daughter exulted in being in charge of the palace and the empire at large, so we are told in the sources that resort to clichés when describing women who overreach. According to the stock scenario, the younger Agrippina was physically attractive and used her charms to lure and then control men. By being overly aggressive and masculine, she became the dominant partner and then emasculated her three husbands in this glimpse of a society spinning out of control. The younger Agrippina, however, attempted to salvage her reputation or, at least, set the record straight, by writing the story of her life. Although the memoir is lost, we know of its existence because it served as a reference for the works of historians. In this Agrippina displays the education and literary background of elite women. Clearly, her memoir demonstrates her awareness of the legacy of the family and her role in history, the particulars of which her mother had instilled in her.

87. Vienna, Kunsthistorisches Museum IX A 63. Gemma Claudia, ca. 50 C.E. The cameo depicts Claudius and the younger Agrippina on the left, and Tiberius and Livia (or, alternately, Germanicus and the elder Agrippina) on the right. The wreathed portraits growing out of cornucopuiae assert the dynastic connection with the depiction of portrait heads all bearing similar features.

Her story has three acts in which she plays the sister of the emperor (Caligula), the wife of the emperor (Claudius), and the mother of the emperor (Nero).

The younger Agrippina's third marriage to the emperor Claudius, her uncle, in 49 C.E. put her on the public stage and gave reign to her considerable talents in politics and administration; in fact, she functioned as a co-ruler in many aspects (Figure 87). Her first concern was to secure a future for her son, Nero, from her first marriage by having Claudius adopt him (she also had Nero betrothed to Claudius's daughter to tie the two families even closer together). In 50 C.E. she received the title *Augusta*, which was closely linked to the adoption in that the title usually honored the mother of a ruling emperor (and not the wife) and evoked dynastic claims to rule (although the implications of the honor were being developed at this time). She had the philosopher Seneca, an old ally, recalled from exile and then appointed him as Nero's tutor. Agrippina took her place beside Claudius in his daily rounds: she participated in the *salutatio* in the palace and even listened to discussions in the senate standing behind a curtain. Matters of finance did not escape her attention as she intervened with a mismanaged public works project and expressed opinions on the complexities of the imperial purse. She had active interests in foreign affairs: she established a colony of veterans at the city in which she was born, later known as Cologne (where the elder Agrippina had accompanied Germanicus on military campaigns), which later looked on her as its patron.

Agrippina's interest in routine aspects of administration did not arouse her enemies as much as her manipulation of the spectacles of the empire. Her assumption of the insignia and prerogatives of imperial power by wearing a golden *chlamys*, a garment of triumphant generals, at certain inaugural ceremonies and her appearance on a *suggestus*, a platform used as a military tribunal, while she received the captive Britons, reportedly indicated her intent to rule. With Claudius's death and Nero's accession in 54 C.E., she at first reigned supremely, but the youthful emperor came into his own and removed his mother from center stage. The woman who had succeeded in the quicksand of Roman politics lost influence over her own son, on whom she had staked everything. Nero allegedly plotted her murder in which she was to drown in a boating accident after a banquet; however, the plan went awry, and he had to send his henchman to stab her to death. In the highly colored account, Agrippina offered her body to her assassins so that they could strike her in the womb that bore Nero, a suitably melodramatic gesture for a scorned mother of this caliber (Tacitus, *Annals*, 14.8). Since the younger Agrippina has come to stand for all that goes wrong when a woman dominates, her reputation as a monstrous female, seducer, commander, and murderer (husbands and rivals allegedly poisoned or executed), precedes her to the extent that is it very difficult to disentangle slander from reality in

the sources. Her portraits as represented on coins and in statuary, however, give no indication of her controversial personality in images that
project a placid and dignified demeanor with the youthful, bland features
commonly found in Julio-Claudian portrait sculpture.

Female leaders emerge in the accounts of conquests of foreign people
labeled as barbarians because of their different customs and ways of living,
which were denigrated as uncivilized and unnatural to Romans. Warrior
queens took on the Roman military in eastern and northern lands. In
Britain the career of Boudicca, who also lived in the mid-first century
C.E., was heroic: as the widow of the client king of Rome in 60–61,
she stood up for the rights of her daughters, who inherited their father's
kingdom jointly with Nero. For this she was flogged and her young
daughters raped, according to Tacitus (*Agricola*, 16.1–2; although Cassius
Dio only refers to payments demanded and loans recalled by Romans
as the cause of the trouble; 62.1–12). A revolt ensued, with Boudicca
leading her troops on the battlefield and sacking cities (including London)
until their defeat by the Roman governor. A description suggests her
power to fascinate both supporters and enemies: "In stature she was
very tall, in appearance most terrifying, her glance was fierce, her voice
harsh; a great mass of the tawniest hair fell to her hips; around her neck
was a large golden torque (neck ring); she wore, as usual, a tunic of
various colors over which a thick mantle was fastened with a brooch,"
(Cassius Dio 62.2 trans. E. Cary). Boudicca nobly committed suicide by
taking poision rather than allowing herself to be taken as a prisoner of
war. In this final act and also in her stirring speeches, she exhibited a
"greater intelligence than often belongs to women" (Cassius Dio 62.2,
trans. E. Cary), a rather high compliment from a historian of the Roman
Empire. Boudicca was depicted as exceptional in her ambition and drive
because only a woman who cultivated the highest male virtues could
aspire to such feats (so she is praised for the masculine aspects of her
character although her political goals were considered treachery). The
story of Boudicca and other warrior women reinforced Roman notions
about women minding their place: when women ruled and fought on
the front lines, they violated the natural order and risked catastrophe for

themselves and their (emasculated) subjects. This lesson was not lost on the imperial women in the capital.

With the suicide of Nero in 68, Rome's first dynasty came to an end. The women of the second dynasty, the Flavians, well represented as artistic subjects on marble portraits and coins, fade from view in the written sources, except for a few notorious scandals involving extramarital affairs. Charges of illicit sexual activity frequently were covers for political misdeeds; yet, the Flavian women apparently did not desire to govern like Livia and the Agrippinas. The wife and niece of Domitian (r. 81–96) appear as victims and viragoes. Julia Titi, daughter of the late emperor Titus (r. 79–81), allegedly was seduced by her uncle Domitian who then forced her to have an abortion that killed her. In the meantime, rumors had it that Domitian was estranged from his wife Domitia because of her affair with an actor, a pantomime artist named Paris, although the imperial couple eventually reconciled. The crimes of incest and adultery, however, point to a political agenda in a campaign to discredit Domitian as an emperor intent on restoring old-fashioned morality (e.g., through reviving the Augustan marriage laws) while corrupting the women of his own house. Domitian's career as a seducer is complemented by Domitia's choice of a lover in a mime artist, the lowest of the low – the contours of both stories conform to the conventions of standard charges against an emperor who dismissed the senate as irrelevant. It is no coincidence that the historians who often provide our only evidence took the senatorial side in these arguments. The story of Domitia's alleged infidelity may conceal a more likely turn of events: Domitian may have tried to banish Domitia for not giving birth to a son (she produced one, but he died very young), but her status as the daughter of a popular general – one martyred by Nero no less – did not give him leeway to remarry at will.

Domitian's affair with Julia probably did not occur. Instead, she may have been a close confidante of the emperor, having lived with him while she was growing up and then residing in the palace after the execution of her husband on political grounds in 82 or 83. After her death in 89 or 90, she was honored by the title *Augusta*, although as daughter of the emperor Titus and niece of his brother Domitian, she left

88. Rome, Museo Nazionale Romano; Erich Lessing/Art Resource, N.Y., 105753. Portrait of Julia Titi, ca. 80–81 C.E. Julia Titi is extraordinarily well represented in the archaeological record as a daughter of an emperor with a shortlived marriage, no children, and a brief life of twenty-six or twenty-seven years. Note the hairstyle associated with the Flavian women that was constructed with the aid of hairpieces – see Figure 64 in Chapter 3. The hairstyle was worn by matrons across the empire in imitation of the imperial women of the Flavian dynasty.

no sons to continue the Flavian dynasty. Julia Titi is depicted in many marble portraits as a maiden whose beauty is all the more poignant to us, no doubt, because of her early demise (Figure 88). Dating from 80–81, the over-lifesize portrait presents a cloud of deeply drilled curls over the forehead and a face characterized by prominent, wide-open eyes, and full lips that curve upward. The extreme symmetry and graceful simplicity of the expressive eyes and mouth reveal that the sculptor did not merely transcribe the looks of Julia Titi but, rather, enhanced or exaggerated features to make the portrait appear even more lovely, that is, idealized. The elaborately styled hair (contrast with Livia's more severe hairstyle; see Figure 82) and the flawless features depend on the sculptor's elegant carving that may have complemented the meticulous grooming of his subject. Produced when Julia Titi was married to a political protégé of Domitan (and before her husband was executed in a political purge), the portrait does not bear any marks of her victimization by the emperor – nor could it in the genre of portraiture that honored its subject. Instead, it presents her as a young woman of the court whose natural beauty is complemented by the elegance of her hairstyle; the curls may have been a hairpiece, which became the height of fashion in the Flavian period. Despite her brief life, there are sufficient examples of the portraits of Julia Titi to suggest her role as a model for young women, who imitated the Flavian coiffure in their own portraits. The so-called affairs of Julia and Domitia recall the role of imperial woman as political pawns, not only to create dynasties and make alliances among aristocratic houses but also to damage the reputation of the men on whom they depended. Imperial women were particularly vulnerable to these charges, and sexual misdeeds were construed as (in this case, alleged) evidence of the emperor's hypocrisy or political incompetency.

The imperial women of the second century were honored for their good works and virtuous characters. Although there were whispers of scandals, the number of these accounts pales in comparison to those of the melodramas of the Agrippinas. As it was not until the mid–second century that an emperor's wife produced an heir as her husband's successor, the responsibilities of motherhood were broadened so that the first lady of Rome became a mother to her country, and her image served to symbolize a host of associated matronly functions. Plotina and Sabina, the wives, respectively, of Trajan (r. 98–117) and Hadrian (r. 117–138), typically were represented on coins decorated with the women's profile on the fronts (the obverse) and a personification or goddess on the backs (the reverse). The tradition of honoring imperial women on coins begins in the first century with the Julio-Claudian dynasty, but in the second century, this evidence becomes more valuable to scholars given the relatively scant literary sources on Plotina and Sabina. Because of the utility and ubiquity of coins, their images were seen by people throughout the empire and many citizens, especially those in remote outposts, would have only recognized the emperor or his wife through their profiles imprinted on money (Figure 89).

89. Poughkeepsie, Frances Lehman Loeb Art Center, Vassar College, CC.59.2.1019. Coin a billon *tetradrachm*, of Hadrian from the mint at Alexandria, Egypt, mid–second century C.E. The coin features a profile bust of Sabina on its reverse. The legend reads, "Sabina Sebasta," in Greek.

In the middle of the second century, the coinage represents a series of personifications to celebrate the fertility of the imperial family as a sign of the times signifying a renewal of Roman society at large (Figures 90 and 91). The prodigious wife who bore fourteen children was the younger Faustina, daughter of the elder Faustina and Antoninus Pius (r. 138–161), who was married to Marcus Aurelius (r. 161–180), the adopted son and successor of Antoninus Pius. The younger Faustina was granted the title of *Augusta* in 146, appropriately a year after her first child was born, and in 174 received the title *Mater Castrorum* (Mother of the Military Camps) as she accompanied Marcus Aurelius on his campaigns (but evidently without intervening on the battlefield as the elder Agrippina was said to have done). The later title evinces the symbolic role of the emperor's wife as mother of her subjects, the Roman people, in aspects appealing to their various constituencies in a time when fewer subjects shared a common identity as Roman (although, paradoxically, Roman citizenship was more widely distributed throughout the empire).

The Roman empire, a peaceable, well-ordered kingdom under Antoninus Pius, encompassed the largest extent of land that it could govern. Shortly thereafter, Marcus Aurelius found himself on the defense against uprisings and incursions along the northern frontiers in Great Britain, German, and Syria (the younger Faustina died with her husband on the eastern frontier in 175). It is striking that in a period of increasing tensions, the legends and personifications on the coins of the realm evoke the powers of the emperor to affect their subjects as if they were all united in kinship and as if each new coin type celebrating the fecundity of Faustina served as a birth announcement to the entire empire. In the early empire, the imperial women come into sharp focus as targets of political attack and invective, while in the second century and later empire, the women appear as generic emblems of domesticity and benevolence in softer focus – in both scenarios, however, the women themselves recede from our view. The filters of imperial ideology were so pervasive that if we could dismiss the (often critical) characterizations of ancient historians and put aside the (idealized or conventionalized) prim or plain-looking portraits on coins or in marble, there is little left to inform us about the imperial women. The task of evaluating their lives requires a skeptical and clear-eyed analysis of the sources: their biases, purposes, and audiences.

Given their range of quasi-official duties, the imperial women retained their high profile in religious affairs throughout the empire, and we turn to the sphere of religion to examine women's involvement in worship, an activity that crossed the boundaries between public and private life and civic and domestic concerns. The religious offices of women as priestesses, the social value of women's cults (that also embraced women of the lower social orders), and their appeal to worshipers in different stages of life will be discussed.

Religious Duties and Sacred Vows

Religion made Roman women visible in the public sphere; participation in processions and offerings got women out of the house, so to speak, and gave some of them jobs in organizing and administrating their cults. It would be difficult, however, to contain the Roman's range of worship and experiences of the sacred to the rather narrow category in which we confine religion. First, the great number and variety of Roman gods and their cults may better compare with the spectrum of worthy causes to which the affluent of today give their time and money, rather than to

90 and 91. Poughkeepsie, Frances Lehman Loeb Art Center, Vassar College, CC. 59.2.0561. Coin, a bronze *sestertius* dating to ca. 161–176 C.E., with a profile of a bust of the younger Faustina on the obverse, and a personification of Felicitas with the legend, *Temporum Felicitas*, Happiness of the Era, on the reverse. The personification holds a child on each arm with two children standing on either side of her and looking up to her on the reverse. Coins with their legends naming the subjects depicted have provided the basis for identifying portrait sculptures that rarely have intact inscriptions on their bases. It has been suggested that Faustina received a new honorary portrait type with the birth of each child, so important was the imperial family as a model.

more familiar notions of worship with an emphasis on commitment to a particular god and sect. Many were the Roman gods and goddesses, with domains highly specialized from state cults governing political protocol and military affairs to those administering agricultural life and the fertility of animals and humans – there were priests who dissected the livers of sacrificed animals for portents of the future and a god of doorways. Romans appealed directly to these gods with offerings, vows, and distinctly forthright appeals, but they also expected something – signs, actions, good fortune – in return for their efforts. There was a religious calendar for the holidays and feast days that shaped the year, but Roman religions lacked sacred texts (except for the Sibylline books, oracles thought to set out the destiny of Rome), so practices depended on tradition and memory. They also did without elite personnel in cults with magistrates and matrons serving as priests and priestesses rather than having a sacred caste that was closer to the gods through their training or

92. Rome, Vatican Museums. Cancelleria Reliefs, Frieze B, scene of Vespasian's return, *adventus*, to Rome, 93–95 C.E. The Vestal Virgin wearing with the signature headdress is the third figure from the left. The Vestals' presence at imperial ceremonies demonstrates their importance. This relief is paired with that of Figure 5 in Chapter 1.

way of living. Although today we tend to see religion as separate from civic life, the Romans emphatically did not.

The public priestesses, known as the Vestal Virgins, occupied a unique position with their extraordinary privileges and proximity to power. Each Vestal served for thirty years (from her appointment when she was between six and ten years old), in which she took a vow of purity that required her to keep the fire in the sacred hearth burning and to remain a virgin. The six Vestals lived in quarters beside their temple at the heart of the Roman Forum because the survival of Rome depended on their vigilance. The legends of early Rome reveal that the hearth fire represented generative power, as noted in accounts in which some of the first kings or founders were conceived by sparks from the ground. As one of the oldest and most venerable colleges of priests (but not the only female one), the Vestals appeared in public with the emperor and his armed guard, the lictors (Figure 92). It is provocative that elements of their costume, the wrapped headdress and plaited coiffure, are similar to those of brides, and others, the long robes and *vittae* (headbands), were worn by matrons because the Vestals were neither nubile maidens nor mothers. Removed from their families and the lot of women, the Vestals were granted other privileges (especially under Augustus), such as the freedom to dispose of their property and make wills without the approval of a guardian, a right for women who have had three children (or four for a freedwoman). It has been pointed out the Vestals functioned as liminal figures; that is, they were betwixt and between the norms for gender and stage of life: they were women who had some of the prerogatives of elite men, yet they remained as virginal daughters. Because many of their sacred duties, like cleaning the storehouse of the temple and preparing the grain that marked sacrificial victims, resembled domestic chores, scholars have sought their origins in their roles of the daughters or wives of the early kings of Rome, but the parallels falter because of their unusual legal powers and regulated sexuality (Figure 93).

The high prestige of the Vestals and the solemnity of their mission are reflected by the punishment allotted Vestals who failed to

93. View of the Temple of Vesta and the Vestals' house in the Roman Forum. Scala/Art Resource, N.Y., 122277.

maintain standards of purity: they were buried alive in several instances in the republic and empire. This extreme and particularly gruesome form of capital punishment may have been considered fitting because of the Vestals' responsibilities in keeping up the hearth in the Forum, a public version of the hearth in private homes that signified well-being, security, and generation through fertility. If the Vestals' house was polluted, then the defenses of the city and empire were weakened. A glance at the rituals in which the Vestals participated indicates their role in promoting the welfare and vitality of the empire through various cults governing aspects of fertility, animal husbandry, and military preparation, and it may be that the Vestal's presence at these rituals reinforced these associations. That the earth should entomb the wanton, living Vestal makes sense in this system of belief.

Most public priesthoods were held by men. Men also administered private religion in the form of the neighborhood cults (the shrine of the crossroads) and domestic worship of the household gods (the *Lares*). As women were excluded from holding political office and serving in the military, they also were forbidden to partake of religious sacrifices. They could neither participate in the slaughtering of animals nor could they prepare the spelt flour (the *mola salsa*) sprinkled on the sacrificial victims. It seems that the Vestals provided the exception that proves the rule, just as the powers of some imperial women may have justified the restrictions placed on women as a group.

Other priesthoods, the *flamen* of Jupiter and the *rex sacrorum* (the king of rites), required its holders to be married, and their wives held complementary priesthoods, the *flaminica Dialis* and the *regina sacrorum* (the queen), who offered regular animal sacrifices. The *flamen* and *flaminica* married in the most traditional and formal rites; the *flaminica* wore her flame-colored bridal veil throughout the years and also made her husband a garment that symbolized their union. The *flaminica* assisted in the rituals that her husband could not perform without her, and if she died, he must resign. Evidently, the priesthood required a level of interdependency. The priestly couple established a model of marital concord and conjugal cooperation, an ideal respected in Rome and in the heavens.

94. Nîmes, Musée Archéologique. Funerary relief of a priestess and military commander, mid–first century C.E. The portrait busts of the dual career couple are framed by a half-niche flanked by dolphins. Their son and daughter commemorated the parents with this fine monument.

Women in the towns of Italy and the provinces served as priestesses. In the eastern empire women could hold public priesthoods of an honorary character; that is, such posts primarily granted women special status, along with the obligation of spending their fortune for the common good (see Plancia Magna in Chapter 1). Such priesthoods were bestowed on prominent citizens who spent less time on strictly religious duties (in our eyes) and rather more money on public relations and civic improvements – the festivals and processions, meals and entertainment, and endowments and building projects that enhanced urban life. A funerary relief of a married couple in Nîmes in southern France displays their commitment to such public service in the titles listed in their inscriptions: Licinia Flavilla is identified in the inscription as a priestess and the wife of Sextus Adgennius Macrinus, a military tribune and a magistrate in the local government (Figure 94; *CIL* 12.3175 and 3368). The husband is depicted wearing his military breastplate as an insignia of his career in the legions, possibly a formative stage of his life. Licinia Flavilla, dressed in the matron's tunic and mantle, displays a coiffure of tight curls over her forehead and long plaits, a hairstyle that is both fashionable and appropriate to her role. Her position probably reflected her high status in the community and required little commitment in comparison to the rigors of the Vestal Virgins' lives. For this couple in the highly Romanized province of south France, the administrative duties and religious titles complemented their social profile of civic and military achievement, prominence, and wealth.

Matrons maintained their own cults that instilled traditional moral values or taught proper deportment in women; that is, elite married women policed their own and also ensured that their social inferiors complied to the cultural norms of behavior (Figure 95). Cults of Venus served as vehicles for social indoctrination, odd as this may seem given Venus's mythological role as goddess of female sexuality or, rather, of erotic attraction and seduction. Yet the goddess had a wider domain in Roman life than is commonly thought, and her many cults assigned all women, from the wives of senators to prostitutes, their place in society. The cult of Venus Obsequens, Venus the Compliant, was established in 295 B.C. when prodigies (frightful or freakish events of nature) occurred after a military victory. After consultation of the Sibylline books, the Temple of Venus Obsequens was built near the Circus Maximus in Rome with money levied as fines against women convicted of adultery. We assume that Venus Obsequens' job was to make the cheating wives yield to custom and to uphold the chastity of their marriages through rituals that brought them under the guidance of upstanding matrons; perhaps by keeping better company in the goddess's temple, the moral rehabilitation of the guilty wives was accomplished. The foundation of the cult follows the contours of many of these tales: the prodigies indicate that something is awry in the relationship between Romans and their gods, the temple is erected to appease the goddess for the poor behavior of her subjects, and the worship performs the social work of accommodating women to their roles. Yet, the establishment of the cult after the successful outcome of war suggests a connection between military action, the domain of men,

95. Boston, Museum of Fine Arts, 34.113. Statue of a Priestess, mid–second century. The woman, standing next to an incense burner in order to make an offering, wears her mantle pulled up over her head as a veil in a manner typical of matrons and a stacked braided coiffure characteristic of priestesses. The signs of advanced age are carefully depicted on the face and neck in the sagging skin and folds of loose flesh. The statue, found in a tomb at Pozzuoli near Naples, commemorates the elderly woman as a devout and dignified priestess.

and the chastity of wives, the defining virtue of matrons. In this case, the wives' lapse disturbed the balance between the sexes: the soldiers were triumphant after the war, while their wives were dishonored. The cult of Venus Obsequens restored the wives from their shameful state through ritual purification and social indoctrination. Ranging from a matron's chastity (defined as fidelity to her husband) to the Vestals' virginity, regulated female sexuality was pivotal to the Roman state and its relationship with its gods.

Another Venus cult ministered to both matrons and prostitutes in a public festival. The cult of Venus Verticordia (the turner of women's

96. Naples, Museo Archeologico Nazionale, inv. 152798. Scala/Art Resource, N.Y., 1274. Statuette of Venus with Priapus, mid–first century C.E. The marble statuette represents the goddess in the act of removing her sandals before she bathes. The figure rests an arm on the head of a small figure of Priapus, the god of sexual arousal, while a tiny Cupid is beneath her foot. Not only was the goddess's jewelry depicted with gilding on the surface of the white marble, but the sandals, a breast band, hair, and pubic hair also were gilded. The statuette was found in a residential and commercial complex, including apartments, a bathhouse, and tavern.

97. Naples, Museo Archeologico Nazionale, inv. 76943. Pair of small bronze cymbals, first century C.E. Cymbals, usually accompanied by tambourines and pipes, provided the music for both cultic and social events. Cymbals kept up the rhythm for dancers who frequently performed at these events.

98. Naples, Museo Archeologico Nazionale, inv. 8924. Scala/Art Resource, N.Y., 47606. Painting depicting the ceremony at the Isis cult, from Herculaneum, first century c.e. The Egyptian cult had a temple in Pompeii, and both men and women (and blacks) participated in the rites of Isis, as seen in this painting. The high priest, flanked by a priestess and another priest with sistra or rattles in hand, begins the rites on the temple porch while the faithful are assembled below on the stairs. Attention is focused on the high priest and his progress toward the lit altar below with the sights and sounds of the spectacle evoked by the white linen robes, shaved male heads, the sistra, and the exotica of ibises and sphinxes.

hearts toward chastity) brought respectable women and those of ill repute together to perform typical cult activities, such as the bathing and adorning of cult statues, and ritual ablutions of worshipers. After cleansing the goddess's statue, the women adorned it with flowers and jewelry (Figures 96, 97, and 98). The women then draped themselves in myrtle wreaths and took baths. The rites concluded with the drinking of a potion made of milk, honey, and poppies. The purpose of these acts, however, was not to purify the women but to make them sexually attractive in order to renew their marriages (for matrons) or to guide them toward marriage (for prostitutes or others of low status). Venus supervised the proceedings that to us may seem more appropriate to a spa than a temple: the women's baths were intended for beautification and self-improvement; during their wash, the women lit incense for another goddess, Fortuna Virilis (male fortune, linked to Venus in the sources) who was to make blemishes on their bodies invisible to their men. Men, although absent from the rites, figure prominently as the recipients of the primping and preening because the cult united women in their appeal to men as sexual partners.

The women worshipers of Venus Verticordia imitated the goddess: they donned myrtle wreaths because Venus had hid herself behind a myrtle bough when satyrs lurked, and they drank the sweet potion Venus sipped when she became a bride. The modesty implied by the myrtle and the prenuptial custom of the drink guided the women worshipers to the duties of the marriage bed. That the rites involve undressing, washing, and decking oneself out, that is, everyday instances of self-maintenance, allowed women to imagine themselves as Venuses who could achieve the physical perfection with which the goddess was endowed (Figure 99). The intimacy of goddess and worshiper is striking, and so is the participation of matrons and prostitutes in the related rites – the collapsing of categories of divinity and mortals and of good women and whores served a ritual function in turning female sexuality to socially productive ends in marriage and childbirth. In the topsy-turvy world of ritual, polite society and the *demimonde* of Rome were mixed together.

Roman religion was especially concerned with matrons, no doubt, because of their role as mothers. Far fewer cults were devoted to young girls or old women, groups without a reproductive capacity, but one goddess who protected maidens on the threshold of womanhood was Diana, whose worship occurred in a celebrated sanctuary on the shores of Lake Nemi, south of Rome. By the first century B.C.E. the temple boasted

99. Rome, Vatican Museums, inv. 936. Statue of a Roman matron in the guise of Venus, late-second century C.E., dedicated to Venus Felix, prosperous Venus, in the inscription on the base. This type of mythological portrait, in which an individualized head is joined to a standard statue type of a divinity, became popular for citizens of the lower social orders in the late first through the second centuries C.E. who honored their loved ones by depicting them in the guise of gods. The cupid at the statue's side may represent the matron's son. The statues were found in a tomb on the outskirts of Rome.

of a gleaming gilt roof, and Augustan poets tell of torchlit processions to the site where women left offerings in the form of textiles or their hair to implore the goddess's aid in marriage and childbirth (Ovid, *Fasti*. 3.269–72; Propertius 2.32.9–10). Nemi, considered a wild place once ruled by a king who had been a fugitive slave, featured woodlands necessary for Diana's passion for the chase, and, in fact, ephebic rites of hunting were held there to prepare young men for their role as warriors and states-men. Diana served primarily as a hunting goddess whose habitat in the wilds and whose aggressive, antisocial nature equipped her to supervise transitions – the passage from youth to adulthood being only one of the debuts that she governed. Diana Nemorensis (Diana of Nemi) has been cast by modern scholars as a protector of girls and young women because of her status as a virgin and comparison with some of the Greek cults of Artemis. Evidence indicates that both boys and girls, men and women, came under the goddess's protection. As one who maimed and killed

100. Nottingham, Castle Museum. Terracotta votives of body parts dedicated at the Sanctuary of Diana at Nemi near Rome, first century B.C.E. Votives serve to focus human and divine attention on the diseased organ in a communication system between mortals and immortals. By leaving models of body parts at the sanctuary, worshipers hoped they would be healed.

through the hunt, Diana also was responsible for healing the wounded. For this reason, the sick and mentally ill requested care and comfort at the sanctuary, the evidence of which can be found in the votives representing the ailing body parts to be treated (Figure 100).

Depicted with arrows, quiver, and dog, Diana the huntress remained an appealing image of fleet-footed grace and adolescent beauty for Roman artists and collectors. The imagery of Diana also was borrowed to commemorate girls who died before their time, that is, before marriage (Figure 101). Girls represented as Diana became ennobled by association after their deaths with the heroic virtues of the hunt and, oddly enough, it was the ambivalence of the huntress, her resistance to categories of gender and mature sexuality, that may have appealed to mourning parents. The ethos of Diana clashed with the ideals of a demure and submissive female demeanor, but her fierce and predatory behavior in the woods

offered an alternate fate to those who died unfulfilled as women, without husbands and children – in other words, the myth offered solace to
grieving parents by providing a transcendent vision of their daughters.
This vision came replete with the hardware of military adventure in the
weaponry and the bracing momentum of action poses to evoke glory,
always a male achievement. The girls, elevated and empowered in these
images, could be seen to partake of the male world of adventure and risk
because they hadn't the chance to develop into women.

Conclusion

Despite their incapacity to perform blood sacrifices, women fully participated in religion from the high priestesses, the Vestals, to matrons who
attended to cults in the home and in the city. Although the processions
and offerings gave some women higher visibility, both state and private

101. Paris, Louvre, MA
1633. Funerary Altar of
Aelia Procula, mid–second
century C.E. The deceased
young girl is depicted in the
disguise of the huntress
Diana. The inscription
informs us that Aelia
Procula's father was an
imperial freedman – AUG.
LIB. – that is, an ex-slave of
the emperor manumitted,
perhaps, to take on a more
important or sensitive post
in the imperial court
(*CIL* 6.*10958*).

cults tended to reinforce traditional values even in instances when the social orders were mixed, as in the rites of Venus Verticordia that momentarily dissolved the social distance between dowagers and prostitutes. Of course, after the conclusion of the rites, the worshipers found themselves back in the everyday world with its rigid norms of behavior, the protocols of which may have appeared even more demanding and stringent to those who enjoyed a brief holiday from them (or, alternatively, reassuring to those for whom the freedom of feast days was chaotically criminal). The sources recount the foundation stories of many of these cults that seem to perform social work, to ground the status quo in "natural" law or heroic tales and to ensure compliance from disenfranchised or marginal groups, such as women, youth, freedmen, and slaves. Women, however, functioned as both actors and audience in religion, as in other aspects of Roman life in which matters of gender intersected with social rank, upbringing, and wealth.

The high public priestesses, the Vestals, followed by the *flaminica Dialis* and the *regina Sacrorum*, who stood apart from the class of women with their prestige and powers, were defined by their relationship to men and, in particular, husbands, in that the Vestals remained nonwives, and the *flaminica* was a form of extreme wife. The Vestals' virginity endowed them with an integrity upon which their powers rested, while the *flaminica's* devotion to archaic customs in her marriage gave her authority. If we ask whether the high priestess's status affected the lot of ordinary women, we would have to say no. They also served neither as models for women nor as mirrors of their social roles because of the very exceptional nature of their positions that enshrined some aspects of feminine domesticity or sexuality but eschewed others. The various cults, public and private, fragmented the image of the female so that we need to look across a wide spectrum of rites in order to get a picture of how Roman religion defined womanhood.

GLOSSARY

Latin and Greek terms italicized

Alumna – a foster-daughter.

Amazon – warrior women in Greek mythology who lived apart from men and outside of social norms.

Andromache – Hector's wife in the Homer's *Iliad*, who remained dignified and beautiful under duress.

Atrium – the central space of a Roman house, often lit from above and surrounded by other rooms.

Augustales – a college of priests consisting of wealthy freedmen. The freedman was given a civic role and social prominence through the official regalia and ceremonial duties required of him in this function.

Benefaction – a charitable gift or service made by a prominent citizen to his or her community.

Clients (*cliens*) – dependents on elite citizens, patrons who assisted and protected them. The patron, in turn, received the loyalty of his clients and their support in political matters or on public occasions.

Chatelaine – a chain to suspend small objects, keys, or cosmetic implements from a woman's garments.

Cognomen – the name usually placed last, that is, the second name for a woman (the third for a man). The first name is a feminine form of her father's family name, the *cognomen* follows, e.g., Gaius Poppaeus Sabinus' daughter was Poppaea Sabina. Families with more than one daughter often distinguished them by using comparative or ordinal adjectives in place of *cognomina (pl.)*: Julia Minor as the younger daughter or Flavia Tertia as the third daughter.

Confarreatio – old-fashioned form of marriage rites celebrated for the wedding of the Flaminica Dialis.

Contubernium – common-law marriages, often between soldiers and their women; literally meaning "shacking-up" (or, rather, "tenting-up" in soldiers' jargon).

Conubium – the legal capacity to marry.

Cultus – refinement or sophistication.

Dacia – the province roughly corresponding to Romania. Its conquest is depicted on the Column of Trajan.

Deductio in domum mariti – the wedding procession that took the bride to her husband's house.

Diva – goddess.

Domus – house.

Dynasties – the succession of emperors based on descendance or bloodties; after Augustus in 14 c.e., his successors from Tiberius through Caligula and Claudius to Nero (68 c.e.) are called the Julio-Claudian dynasty. The Flavian dynasty (69–96 c.e.) consisted of Vespasian and his two sons, Titus and Domitian. The Antonine dynasty began with Antoninus Pius and followed with Marcus Aurelius and Lucius Verus, and Commodus (138–192 c.e.). The Severan dynasty consisted of Septimius Severus and his son Caracalla (who had ordered the murder of his younger brother Geta; the Severans ruled from 193–217 c.e.).

Encaustic – painting in which the pigments are suspended in melted wax.

Epigraphy – the study of inscriptions.

Etruscans – people who ruled central Italy in a series of city-states in the eighth through fourth centuries B.C.E.

Fayum – fertile district of farmland in Egypt south of Alexandria; the mummy portraits take this name even though they came from other areas in Egypt as well.

Filia – daughter.

Freedwoman – a slave who has been manumitted to become a citizen.

Hellenism – the culture of Classical Greece, which was accorded great respect and prestige by elite Romans, although it remained suspect as irrevocably foreign, pompous, and useless by various groups in different periods.

Infamis – notorious, disreputable, of ill-repute.

Insula – a city block, although frequently refers to a multidwelling building or apartment house.

Italic – characterizes the early peoples of central Italy before Romanization.

Kline – a couch, either used for dining or sleeping (and represented in funerary art as furniture in which the dead are laid to rest).

Laudatio Turiae – a public eulogy delivered by a husband in honor of his wife, Turia, in 10–9 B.C.E. Turia acted bravely on behalf of her family and husband in the violent years of the late republic while also demonstrating the appropriate domestic virtues (*CIL* 6.1527).

Matrona (*matrona*) – respectable married woman.

Manus – defines the type of marriage a woman enters; in early Rome, a bride entered into a marriage with *manus* in which she came under the authority of her husband or his father; in the late republic and later, she typically married without *manus* so that she remained a member of her father's family.

Materfamilias – mother, female head of the household.

Meretrix – whore.

Negotium – the official duties of the ruling class.

Nubere – to veil oneself, as the bride does for her wedding day.

Numismatics – the study of coins.

Paedagogus – childminder, a slave whose job it was to attend to children.

Papyri – documents written on sheets that were made from strips of the stems of the papyrus plant. The process entailed pressing the strips together to make sheets for writing. Many of these were preserved in the dry sands of Roman Egypt, thus, providing invaluable archives of legal and financial documents, as well as personal letters.

Parthia – the land originally corresponding to Iran, but later extending its empire further north and east into Central Asia. Parthia remained a traditional enemy of Rome.

Patria Potestas – the father's absolute legal rights over the members of his househould.

Paterfamilias – the father, head of the household.

Princeps – first among equals or leader. A title used by Augustus.

Pudicitia – chastity as a virtue for women and, more particularly, as fidelity to the marriage bond for a matron.

Sarcophagus – a marble box, usually carved in relief on the exterior, used as a coffin.

Salutatio – the morning rounds of visits to great men's houses.

Scroll – the ancient form of the book.

Stola – a matron's garment worn over her tunic and hung from the shoulders by straps.

Strategos – military and political leader in Greek cities.

Sumptuary laws – legislation limiting women's rights to wear showy garments and jewelry in public.

Togate – toga-wearing; the identifying garment of a Roman citizen.

Tutela – guardianship for women who were not under the authority of their fathers or husbands; guardians looked after women's financial and legal transactions.

Univira – a woman who had been married only once, literally a "one-man woman."

ROMAN AUTHORS

Apuleius (ca. 125–170 C.E.): Born in north Africa, he wrote a novel called the *Metamorphoses* (known as *The Golden Ass*), a tale of adventure, magic, and religious conversion.

Cassius Dio (ca. 164- after 229 C.E.): A provincial citizen from Turkey who entered the senate and reached high office in Rome. He is known for his Roman history covering early Rome to 229 C.E.

Catullus (ca. 84–54 B.C.E.): Author of poems (elegies) that reflect upon friendship, love, and the life of the sentiments and mind.

Cicero (106–43 B.C.E.): Roman statesman and senator who was also a prodigious writer of letters, philosophical treatises, forensic speeches (that of the forum and its law courts), and other works.

Favorinus of Arles (ca. 85–155 C.E.): Writer and performer of the Second Sophistic, which revived Greek learning, rhetoric, and myth in the second century.

Galen (ca. 129?–199/216 C.E.): Starting out as a doctor for gladiators in Pergamum, he climbed to the position of court physician to Marcus Aurelius in Rome. He wrote both philososphical and medical treatises.

Gellius (ca. 125–late second century C.E.): The author of *Attic Nights*, a collection of thoughts on diverse subjects allegedly composed in the evenings of a winter spent near Athens.

Horace (65–8 B.C.E.): Poet of the Augustan age whose work ranges from more personal and idiosyncratic topics to broad themes of patriotic fervor.

Juvenal (active in late first–early second centuries C.E.): Wrote satires attacking the foibles of Roman society marked by broad observation, although laced generously with polemic and invective.

Livy (59 B.C.E.–17 C.E.): Author of a Roman history from the beginnings of Rome to the reign of Augustus.

Lucretius (ca. 98–55 B.C.E.): Wrote a didactic poem, *De Rerum Natura*, on Epicurean principles, the study of nature and man's ability to achieve higher states of happiness through reason.

Martial (ca. 38 or 41–104 C.E.): Wrote epigrams, brief witty poems on people, places, and events in his life, in which urbane Roman society was served up in a panorama of social types.

Musonius Rufus (ca. 30–101 C.E.): A Stoic philosopher.

Ovid (43 B.C.E.–17 C.E.): Poet whose works focus on love elegy (the worldly cares of young men and women), and Greek myth, among other topics. In A.D. 8, Augustus punished Ovid by sending him to live near the Black Sea. The official cause was said to have been the immorality of his poetry (especially the *Ars Amatoria* or *The Art of Love*), but his involvement in the adultery of Augustus's daughter, Julia, was also suspected.

Petronius (active in mid–first century C.E.): Author of the *Satyricon*, a novel recounting the adventures and mishaps of a wandering hero. The *Satyricon* also provides a caricature of the rich and vulgar freedman, Trimalchio, and his wife, Fortunata.

Plautus (active ca. 205–184 B.C.E.): Writer of comic plays, known as New Comedy, which featured stock character types (most characteristic of these are the clever slave), and formulaic plots that turn on cases of mistaken identity and thwarted desires for love or lust or money.

Pliny the Elder (ca. 23–79 C.E.): Held important administrative positions under Vespasian and wrote *The Natural History*, an exhaustive encyclopedia on subjects ranging from geography, zoology to metallurgy and mineralogy (including a section on the history of art).

Pliny the Younger (61 or 62–113 C.E.): Nephew of Pliny the Elder, who had a career in law and politics. His collection of *Epistulae*, letters in ten books, gives a sense of fashionable society, literary ambitions, and the routines of large landowners of his day.

Plutarch (before 50–after 120 C.E.): Philosopher and biographer from Greece whose *Lives* of great men focus on their virtues. He paired biographies of Greek and Roman leaders to suggest the complementary relationship of Greek intellectual traditions and Roman statecraft.

Propertius (ca. 54 or 47–after 16 B.C.E. or until 2 C.E.): Wrote four books of elegies, many of which recount his love affair with Cynthia, a cultured and freewheeling woman of the *demimonde*.

Soranus (ca. 98–138 C.E.): A physician from Ephesus who studied in Alexandria and worked in Rome. Of his books, his work on gynecology is important for the light it sheds on Roman attitudes and practices.

Suetonius (ca. 70–130 C.E.): An imperial administrator who wrote biographies ("lives") of the emperors.

Sulpicia (later first century B.C.E.): Niece of the jurist Servius Sulpicius and Messalla Corvinus, a politician who was a patron of other poets. Several of her elegies about her love of Cerinthus have been preserved in a collection atrributed to another poet.

Tacitus (56–ca. 120 C.E.): Senator and author of histories of the early empire who looked backed on republican Rome with nostalgia and viewed many of the emperors of the first century C.E. as weakened and wayward leaders. He cast their women as corrupting influences, scheming and plotting for their own ends, rather than for the good of Rome.

Valerius Maximus (active in early first century C.E.): Wrote a handbook of models of virtues and vices for use in rhetorical schools.

Varro (116–27 B.C.E.): A man of incomparable learning and antiquarian interests, Varro wrote works on language and literary history, history and geography, rhetoric and law, and philosophy and science. His *De Re Rustica* discusses agricultural life from the point of view of the country gentleman, the owner of villas and large estates.

Virgil (70–19 B.C.E.): The great poet of the Augustan age whose epic poem, *The Aeneid*, celebrated Rome's founder and its past.

SELECT BIBLIOGRAPHY

Allason-Jones, L. (1989). *Women in Roman Britain*. London: British Museum Publications.

Barrett, A. A. (2002). *Livia: First Lady of Imperial Rome*. New Haven and London: Yale University Press.

Barrett, A. A. (1996). *Agrippina. Sex, Power, and Politics in the Early Empire*. New Haven and London: Yale University Press.

Beard, M. (1995). "Re-reading (Vestal) Virginity," in R. Hawley and B. Levick, eds. *Women in Antiquity: New Assessments*. London and New York: Routledge: 166–177.

Beard, M. (1980). "The Sexual Symmetry of Vestal Virgins." *Journal of Roman Studies* 70:12–27.

Beard, M., J. North, and S. Price, eds., (1998). *Religions of Rome*. Cambridge and New York: Cambridge University Press, vols. 1–2.

Boatwright, M. T. (1991). "The Imperial Women of the Early Second Century A.D." *American Journal of Philology* 112:513–540.

Bodel, J., ed. (2001). *Epigraphic Evidence: Ancient History from Inscriptions*. London and New York: Routledge.

Bradley, K. R. (1991). *Discovering the Roman Family. Studies in Roman Social History*. Oxford: Oxford University Press.

Braund, S. (1992). "Juvenal – Misognyist or Misogamist?" *Journal of Roman Studies* 82:71–86.

Bremen, R. Van. (1996). *The Limits of Participation. Women and Civic Life in the Greek East in the Hellenistic and Roman Periods.* Amsterdam: J. G. Gieben.

Brown, R. (1995). "Livy's Sabine Women and the Ideal of Concordia." *Transactions of the American Philological Association* 125:291–319.

Clarke, J. R. (1998). *Looking at Lovemaking: Constructions of Sexuality in Roman Art, 100 B.C.–A.D. 250.* Berkeley and Los Angeles: University of California Press.

Conte, G. B. (1994). *Latin Literature: A History*, trans. J. B. Solodow. Baltimore and London: Johns Hopkins University Press.

Culham, P. (1997). "Did Roman Women Have an Empire?" in M. Golden and P. Toohey, eds., *Inventing Ancient Culture.* London and New York: Routledge, 192–204.

D'Ambra, E. (2006). "Daughters as Diana in Mythological Portraiture," in S. Bell and I. S. Hansen, eds., *Role Models: Cultural Assimilation and Identity in the Roman World and Early Modern Italy* (forthcoming University of Michigan Press).

D'Ambra, E. (1998). *Roman Art.* Cambridge and New York: Cambridge University Press.

D'Ambra, E. (1996). "The Calculus of Venus: Nude Portraits of Roman Matrons," in N. B. Kampen, ed., *Sexuality in Ancient Art.* Cambridge and New York: Cambridge University Press, 219–232.

Dawid, M. (2003). *Die Elfenbeinplastiken aus dem Hanghaus 2 in Ephesos: Räume SR 18 und SR 28.* Vienna: Österreichischen Akademie der Wissenschaften.

Delia, D. (1991). "Fulvia Reconsidered," in S. B. Pomeroy, ed., *Women's History and Ancient History.* Chapel Hill: University of North Carolina Press, 197–217.

Dixon, S. (2001). *Reading Roman Women.* London: Duckworth.

Dixon, S. (1992). *The Roman Family.* Baltimore and London: Johns Hopkins University Press.

Dixon, S. (1988). *The Roman Mother.* Norman and London: University of Oklahoma Press.

Fantham, E., H. P. Foley, N. B. Kampen, S. B. Pomeroy, and H. A. Shapiro, eds. (1994). *Women in the Classical World*. Oxford and New York: Oxford University Press.

Fischler, S. (1994). "Social Stereotypes and Historical Analysis: The Case of Imperial Women at Rome," in L. J. Archer, S. Fischler, and M. Wycke, eds. *Women in Ancient Societies: An Illusion of the Night*. London: Macmillan.

Flemming, R. (2000). *Medicine and the Making of Roman Women*. Oxford: Oxford University Press.

Flory, M. B. (1993). "Livia and the History of Public Honorific Statues for Women in Rome," *Transactions of the American Philological Association* 123:287–308.

Flower, H., ed. (2004). *The Cambridge Companion to the Roman Republic*. Cambridge and New York: Cambridge University Press.

Flower, H. (2002). "Were Women Ever 'Ancestors' in Republican Rome?" in J. M. Højte, ed. *Images of Ancestors*. Aarhus: Aarhus University Press, 159–184.

Forbis, E. P. (1996). *Municipal Virtues in the Roman Empire. The Evidence of Italian Honorary Inscriptions*. Stuttgart-Leipzig: B. G. Teubner.

Fraschetti, A., ed. (2001). *Roman Women*, trans L. Lappin. Chicago and London: University of Chicago Press.

Gardner, J. F. (1998). *Family and Familia in Roman Law and Life*. Oxford: Clarendon Press.

Gardner, J. F. (1986). *Women in Roman Law and Society*. Bloomington: Indiana University Press.

George, M. (2000). "Family and Familia on Roman Biographical Sarcophagi." *Mitteilungen des Deutschen Archäologischen Institut, Römische Abteilung* 107:191–207.

Goldsworthy, A. (2003). *The Complete Roman Army*. London: Thames and Hudson.

Gourevitch, D., and M.-T. Raepsaet-Charlier (2001). *La femme dans la Rome antique*. Paris: Hachette.

Hallett, J. P. (1997). "Female Homoeroticism and the Denial of Roman Reality in Latin Literature," in J. P. Hallett and M. Skinner, eds., *Roman Sexualities*. Princeton, NJ: Princeton University Press, 255–73.

Hallett, J. P. (1984). *Fathers and Daughters in Roman Society: Women and the Elite Family*. Princeton, NJ: Princeton University Press.

Hemelrijk, E. (1999). *Matrona Docta: Educated Women in the Roman Elite from Cornelia to Julia Domna*. London and New York: Routledge.

Hopkins, K. (1993). "Novel Evidence for Roman Slavery." *Past and Present* 138:3–25.

James, Sharon L. (2003). *Learned Girls and Male Persuasion: Gender and Reading in Roman Love Elegy*. Berkeley and Los Angeles: University of California Press.

Joshel, S. R. (1992). *Work, Identity, and Legal Status at Rome. A Study of the Occupational Inscriptions*. Norman and London: University of Oklahoma Press.

Kampen, N. B. (1981). *Image and Status: Roman Working Women in Ostia*. Berlin: Mann.

Keith, A. M. (2000). *Engendering Rome: Women in Latin Epic*. Cambridge and New York: Cambridge University Press.

Keith, A. M. (1997). "*Tandem venit amor*: A Roman Woman Speaks of Love," in J. P. Hallett and M. B. Skinner, eds., *Roman Sexualities*. Princeton: Princeton University Press, 295–310.

Kleiner, D. E. E. (1992). *Roman Sculpture*. New Haven and London: Yale University Press.

Kleiner, D. E. E. (1987). *Roman Imperial Funerary Altars with Portraits*. Rome: Bretschneider.

Kleiner, D. E. E., and S. Matheson, eds. (2000). *I, Claudia, II: Women in Roman Art and Society*. Austin: University of Texas Press.

Kleiner, D. E. E., and S. Matheson, eds. (1996). *I, Claudia: Women in Ancient Rome*. Austin: University of Texas Press.

Leach, Eleanor Winsor. (2004). *The Social Life of Painting in Ancient Rome and on the Bay of Naples*. Cambridge and New York: Cambridge University Press.

MacMullen, R. (1986). "Women's Power in the Principate," *Klio* 68: 434–443.

MacMullen, R. (1980). "Women in Public in the Roman Empire," *Historia* 28:108–118.

Olson, K. (2002). "*Matrona* and Whore: The Clothing of Women in Roman Antiquity." *Fashion Theory* 6:387–420.

Parkin, T. G. (1992). *Demography and Roman Society*. Baltimore and London: Johns Hopkins University Press.

Phillips, J. E. (1978). "Roman Mothers and the Lives of their Adult Daughters," *Helios* 6:68–80.

Pomeroy, S. B. (1976). "The Relationship of the Married Woman to Her Blood Relatives in Rome," *Ancient Society* 7:215–227.

Purcell, N. (1986). "Livia and the Womanhood of Rome," *Papers of the Cambridge Philological Society* 212, n.s., 32:78–105.

Rawson, B. (2003). *Children and Childhood in Roman Italy*. Oxford: Oxford University Press.

Rawson, B., ed. (1991). *Marriage, Divorce and Children in Ancient Rome*. Canberra-Oxford: Clarendon Press.

Rawson, B., and P. R.C. Weaver, eds. (1997). *The Roman Family in Italy. Status, Sentiment, Space*. Canberra-Oxford: Clarendon Press.

Richlin, A. (1997). "Pliny's Brassiere," in J. P. Hallett and M. B. Skinner, eds. *Roman Sexualities*. Princeton, NJ: Princeton University Press, 197–220.

Richlin, A. (1981). "Approaches to the Sources on Adultery at Rome," *Women's Studies* 8:225–250.

Rowlandson, J., ed. (1998). *Women and Society in Greek and Roman Egypt: A Sourcebook*. Cambridge and New York: Cambridge University Press.

Saller, R. P. (1994). *Patriarchy, Property and Death in the Roman Family*. Cambridge and New York: Cambridge University Press.

Scheid, J. (2003). *An Introduction to Roman Religion*, trans. By J. Lloyd. Bloomington and Indianapolis: Indiana University Press.

Scheid, J. (1992). "Religious Roles of Roman Women," in P. Schmitt Pantel, ed., *A History of Women: From Ancient Goddesses to Christian Saints*. Cambridge, MA: Harvard University Press: 377–408.

Sebesta, J. L., and L. Bonfante, eds. (1994). *The World of Roman Costume*. Madison and London: University of Wisconsin Press.

Setälä, P., and L. Savunen, eds. (1999). *Female Networks and the Public Sphere in Roman Society*. Rome: Acta Instituti Romani Finlandiae.

Shaw, B. (1991). "The Cultural Meanings of Death: Age and Gender in the Roman Famly," in D. Kertzer and R. P. Saller, eds., *The Family in Italy from Antiquity to the Present*. New Haven and London: Yale University Press, 66–90.

Shaw, B. (1987). "The Age of Roman Girls at Marriage: Some Reconsiderations," *Journal of Roman Studies* 77:30–46.

Staples, A. (1997). *From Good Goddess to Vestal Virgins. Sex and Category in Roman Religion*. London and New York: Routledge.

Stehle, E. (1989). "Venus, Cybele, and the Sabine Women: The Roman Construction of Female Sexuality," *Helios* 16.2:143–164.

Treggiari, S. (1991). *Roman Marriage. Iusti Coniuges from the Time of Cicero to the Time of Ulpian*. Oxford: Oxford University Press.

Treggiari, S. (1979). "Lower Class Women in the Roman Economy," *Florilegium* 1:65–86.

Treggiari, S. (1976). "Jobs for Women," *American Journal of Ancient History* 1:76–104.

Vinson, M. P. (1987). "Domitia Longina, Julia Titi, and the Literary Tradition," *Historia* 38:431–450.

Virgili, P., and C. Viola, eds. (1990). *Bellezza e seduzione nella Roma imperiale*. Rome: De Luca Edizioni d'Arte.

Walker, S., and M. Bierbrier, eds. (1997). *Ancient Faces: Mummy Portraits from Roman Egypt*. London: British Museum Press.

Wood, S. (1999). *Imperial Women: A Study in Public Images, 40 B.C.–A.D. 68*. Leiden: Brill.

Wyke, M. (2002). *The Roman Mistress: Ancient and Modern Representations*. Oxford: Oxford University Press.

INDEX

Venus, 4, 6, 25, 75, 153, 177
  And Mars, 155
  Bathing, 7
  Venus Felix, 177
Verginia, 26, 32, 59
Vespasian, 36
  Return of, 168
Vestal Virgins, 9, 31, 74, 153, 168–170, 172, 180
  Did not serve as models, 180
  Dress and hair, 168
  Keeping of the fire, 168
  Liminal figures, 168
  Military preparation, 170
  Pollution of house, 170
  Punishment, 169
    Buried alive, 170
  Sacred hearth, 168, 170
    Generative power of, 168
    Symbol of generation through fertility, 170
  Temple of, 168
  Vow of purity, 168, 169, 180
Vesuvius, 103
Veteran, 40
  Conflict over land for, 148
Via di Diana, 102
Victory monument, 42
Viminal Hill, 82
Vindolanda, 129, 132
Virgil, 9
Virtue, 63
  Wifely, 58
Votives, 178
Vulci, 57

Wagon, 109, 133
  Covered, 133

Fitted with beds, 133
  Miniature, 109
Warfare, 13
Warrior, 177
Water, 76
Waxed *Tabula*, 96
Weakness, 12
Wealth, 27, 31, 48, 49, 60, 95, 128
  Of women
    Display of, 144
Weavers, 99
Weaving, 94, 97, 100, 149
Wedding, 69, 73–76
Wedding finery, 68
Wedding plans, 66
Widows, 13, 46, 72
Wifely devotion, 81
Wigs, 112–113, 119, 123
  Marble, 120
Wills, 24, 52
Wine, 47, 55
Wisdom, 68
Witchcraft, 87
Wives, 9, 11, 34, 47, 48, 50, 51
  Adulterous, 48
Women, 133
  Aging, 176
  As monsters, 143
  Badge of honor of, 112
  Daily rounds, 33
  of ill repute, 175
  Quarters of, 96
  Respectable, 175
Wool, 58, 60, 76
Wool-basket, 60
Wool spinning, 147
Woolweighers, 99
Woolworkers, 99

For EU product safety concerns, contact us at Calle de José Abascal, 56–1°,
28003 Madrid, Spain or eugpsr@cambridge.org.

www.ingramcontent.com/pod-product-compliance
Ingram Content Group UK Ltd.
Pitfield, Milton Keynes, MK11 3LW, UK
UKHW020308140625
459647UK00014B/1797